Innovating for competitive advantage in the legal profession

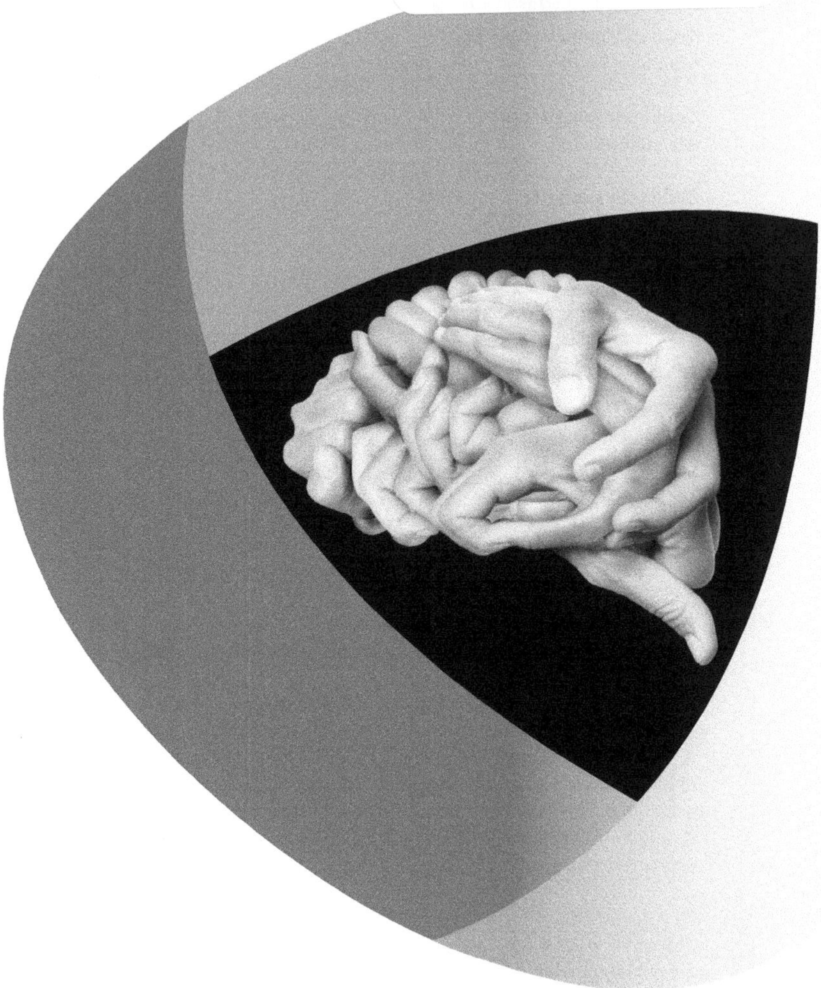

EDITED BY ALEX DAVIES

Head of events and books
Leah Darbyshire

Commissioning editor
Alex Davies

Editorial assistant
Francesca Ramadan

Published by
Globe Law and Business Ltd
3 Mylor Close
Horsell
Woking
Surrey GU21 4DD
United Kingdom
Tel: +44 20 3745 4770
www.globelawandbusiness.com

ISBN: 978-1-78358-342-3
A catalogue record for this book is available from the British Library

Contents

Executive summary

Innovation – it's the word on everyone's lips. How to go about it, what it can do for your business – what even is it? Can innovation be applied in the legal environment?

Such is the interest and appetite for legal innovation that, in the last 18 months, ARK has published over a dozen titles with innovation in their remit, covering everything from knowledge management to pricing, from marketing to recruitment, and everything in between. This compilation deep-dives into the key areas that drive innovation forward in the legal profession, combining the views and experiences of 14 leaders in their fields.

Why do we need an innovation agenda? Where and how do we start? What are the common scenarios which drive innovation and what should determine our approach? The opening chapter of this book, by barrister Duncan Hart, aims to answer all these questions, including determining the values, behaviors, and processes that provide the foundations of innovation for the leadership team to build upon to bring such an agenda forward.

Chapter 2, by Markus Hartung and Arne Gärtner at Bucerius Law School, Hamburg, provides an overview of disruptive innovation in the legal service industry. While new market entrants do in some cases have the potential to replace at least parts of the traditional law firm service offering – a threat to "traditional" providers that is only going to increase – it is the companies who foot the bill for both "traditional" and "alternative" providers who will ultimately be responsible for driving the future of innovation in the legal industry.

While law firms strive to extract more work from their clients, general counsel are under greater pressure to keep more work inhouse and to prove their value through visible revenue growth. In chapter 3, Deepa Tharmaraj, legal director at Dell, looks at why creativity and innovation are the key to value enhancement for legal departments, and provides the in-house perspective on innovation and growth in a lean in-house legal department.

Chapter 4 describes the foundations on which a firm can build a more systematic and intentional approach to innovation. Adam Billing and Abigail Hunt from Møller PSF Group describe the barriers firms are likely to encounter, and how these may be overcome.

Duncan Hart returns to author chapter 5, looking at the tangible and intangible aspects of a law firm and its people that encourage innovation. Chapter 6 then explores the reasons why law firms fail to meet client expectations, and how this can negatively impact the firm's performance and profitability. Drawing from inside experience from both in-house counsel and law firm departments, Chris Howe, director at Raedbora Consulting and a lead advisor at DealScoper.com, looks at how clients are beginning to force the pace on innovation, and what it will take for firms to be a winner rather than a loser.

Chapter 7, by Mark Gould, founder of Mark Gould Consulting, looks specifically at how knowledge management – which in most law firms is geared towards improving access to knowledge or expertise – can instead be leveraged to create a culture where innovation is part of the fabric of the firm.

Moving on to the theme of technology, chapter 8 looks at the role of technological innovation, and how it has played an important role in slowly reshaping the way in which lawyers conduct their profession. Emerging technologies, says J Stephen Poor, chair emeritus at Seyfarth Shaw, promise a deeper and more fundamental change in the way in which lawyers operate. This chapter reviews the historical context of the industry's relationship with technology, and discusses the current stage of technological innovation. Stephen then offers perspectives on how new technologies can augment the role of people and work to reshape or enhance the attorney/client relationship.

Simon Nash, director at Insight Limited, discusses in chapter 9 how the law has evolved over time leading to lawyers preferring innovation in small increments. However, in every generation there are one or two individuals, or firms, who redefine an area of practice with a bold paradigmatic change of the sort one more commonly expects to find in sectors such as tech or investment banking. When those changes are successful, they set the scene for the next phase of incrementalism within that new paradigm. This chapter shows how practices of different sizes have sought to innovate their reward structures, demonstrating how solid management outcomes can be achieved, whether in terms of the Maister model variables of margin, pricing, utilization, and leverage, or through a psychological analysis of extrinsic and intrinsic work motivators.

This chapter leads nicely to a series of three case studies on innovation in law firms. In the first, Scott Rechtschaffen from Littler Mendelson, argues that a true innovation strategy "envisions dramatically and comprehensively changing the way firms interact with and serve their clients". The case study describes how Littler Mendelson has used innovation as a game-changer over the past two decades and how KM can be the foundation of a comprehensive content marketing strategy.

In the second, Oz Benamram and Kathy Skinner reflect on how White & Case became a hostage in a vendor relationship and used innovation to find a solution. With reference to the suppliers of legal information and change management, Benamram and Skinner describe how White & Case has optimized its research tools to deliver value through increased efficiency and – interestingly – reduction of costs to clients.

For employees to feel truly engaged with a business, their values must be aligned with those of the organization so that they derive meaning from their work – so says Michael Bradley of Marque Lawyers. In the third of the case studies, the managing partner of the Sydney-based firm candidly talks about the pressures in the legal marketplace, the values that drive Marque Lawyers and set it apart, and explains why it's an exciting time to be a lawyer – for those who can see past the threats to the opportunities of an overcrowded market.

Two final chapters complete this compilation on innovation. John Alber, legal futurist at the ITLA, dives deep into Design Thinking and explains how this empathy-based approach to innovation can be applied to legal service design, illustrating his chapter with successful examples from within and outside the legal sector. Finally, Duncan Hart concludes the book with practical lessons for law firms wanting to engage in innovation.

About the authors

John Alber serves as futurist for the Institute for Future of Law Practice. He was also the first futurist for the International Legal Technology Association. He writes, speaks and consults widely, focusing on finding practical ways to reshape the delivery of legal services to suit a future demanding excellence far beyond substantive legal skills. Prior to his current role, John was a transportation industry CEO. Thereafter, he led Bryan Cave LLP to become one of the most innovative firms in the world, serving as its strategic innovation partner for more than 16 years. While at Bryan Cave, he also served for seven years on the firm's operating group (its management committee). At Bryan Cave, John created one of the first Practice Economics consulting groups, one of the client facing technology groups and one of the first in-firm legal process outsourcing (LPO) organizations. The groups he created developed innovative web-based, client-centric applications that delivered legal advice to clients, managed complex workflows and even created pleadings automatically. They also developed client-facing knowledge management, project management, project estimation and business intelligence systems and highly technology-leveraged alternative staffing solutions for engagements of all types. John is an Emeritus fellow of the College of Law Practice Management. He has received a number of awards, both in the legal field and in information technology generally. Among other awards, he received ILTA's first ever Premiership Award, was named American Lawyer Media's first ever "Champion of Technology", was given a Lifetime Achievement Award by Law Technology News and recognized as one of the Top 25 CTOs in the world by Infoworld. In addition, while under his leadership, Bryan Cave received recognition as a CIO Magazine "Top 100 Company" and was twice recognized as ILTA's Most Innovative Firm.

Oz Benamram is chief knowledge officer at White & Case, providing the firm with strategic direction on the use of KM and technology. He leads the knowledge department in developing and implementing the systems and processes that enable the firm to use its collective knowledge to benefit clients worldwide. Oz is a globally recognized thought leader and a frequent speaker on legal IT and KM subjects. He has won numerous awards for leading innovation in legal KM, including the creation of an enterprise search system.

Adam Billing is the founder of Treehouse Innovation (www.treehouseinnovation.com). He works with leading corporate and professional service organisations, helping them to develop new products, services, and strategy, and to build their own internal innovative capacity.

Michael Bradley is the managing partner of Marque Lawyers, a boutique commercial law firm in Sydney which he and some fellow refugees from Big Law founded in 2008 with the stated intention of completely revolutionizing the way law is practiced. Anyone who has had anything to do with Marque will attest that it really does do law differently. Apart from continuing to explore how much fun a lawyer can have while pretending to work, Michael writes regularly on public interest issues, the legal industry, and whatever else he gets excited about. He also wrote a book called *Kill all the Lawyers*, which pretty much sums it all up.

Dr Arne Gärtner is a senior legal project manager at Linklaters. As manager of the firm's German Business Improvement team, he is also generally responsible for Legal Project Management (LPM) and Legal Technology (LT) in Germany. In his role as a senior LPM he supports the practice in the management of large and complex matters and advises on the use of technology for handling such transactions. Furthermore, Arne is a member of the global Innovation and Efficiency working group of Linklaters and responsible for Innovation and Efficiency in Germany.

Arne studied Business Administration at the University of Potsdam and Mediation at the European University of Viadrina Frankfurt (Oder). He also holds a PhD in Business Administration from the University of Potsdam. In addition, he is an IPMA (International Project Management Association) certified Project Management Associate and Fellow of the Bucerius Center on the Legal Profession where he worked as a Research Assistant from 2012 till 2015.

Mark Gould is the founder of Mark Gould Consulting, a business focused on helping law firms use their knowledge more productively. He works with firms of all sizes, helping them to stand out in their markets by acting as a catalyst for improvement, combining his understanding of the legal sector with the firm's deep knowledge. He was head of knowledge management at Addleshaw Goddard LLP between 2006 and 2014, and a PSL at the same firm from 2001. Prior to that, he spent 13 years teaching law at the University of Bristol.

Duncan Hart practiced as a barrister and solicitor for over 20 years before becoming the regional managing director of one of Australasia's largest firms with over 2,000 employees. He became a full-time consultant in 2002. His various consultancies have taken him from Silicon Valley to Shanghai, and his clients include not only law firms, but a wide cross-section of industry groups, including manufacturing, health, education, and IT.

Duncan's first book, *The Strategic Law Firm* (Ark Group, 2010), argued the case for a more strategic approach to law firm management, and in particular the adoption of the types of strategic planning tools and methodologies that he had seen in operation in many of his clients' industry sectors.

More recently, his background in intellectual property has led him to explore more closely the role of disruptive technologies and business models in various sectors, including law, patent attorney, and other professions. Many of his recent assignments involve the so-called "start-up" sector, and larger more mature industries where clients are seeking to develop innovation-based strategies in fields as diverse as bio-tech and logistics.

In all his assignments, Duncan draws from a rich palette of industry and professional experience, and he is committed to the belief that law firms, like any other business, have much to learn from other sectors, particularly in the area of innovation-based strategy. In short, they should be encouraged to experiment to find new, and hopefully better, solutions for both the firm and their clients.

Markus Hartung is a lawyer and mediator. He is director of the Bucerius Center on the Legal Profession (CLP) at Bucerius Law School, Hamburg. His expertise in the framework of the CLP lies in market development and trends, management and strategic leadership, as well as corporate governance of law firms and business models of law firms with regard to digitalisation of the legal market. He is chair of the committee on professional regulation of the German Bar Association (DAV).

As a lawyer he focuses on conflict management, regulatory matters and professional indemnity issues. In addition, he advises law firms in strategy and management questions and coaches partners in management functions. He is a regular lecturer and conference-speaker on leadership, management topics, and professional ethics and has written numerous articles and book chapters on these topics. He is co-editor and author of *Wegerich/Hartung: Der Rechtsmarkt in Deutschland (The Legal Market in Germany)* which came to the market in early 2014 and has developed into a standard reference for the German legal market. He is also co-author of *How Legal Technology Will Change the Business of Law*, a joint study of The Boston Consulting Group and the Bucerius Law School. His recently published book Legal Tech. *Die Digitalisierung des Rechtsmarkts* is the first comprehensive analysis of the impact of legal technology on the legal profession in German speaking countries.

Chris Howe is a director of Raedbora Consulting. In his consulting role he advises legal clients on pricing and practice management (including restructuring and day-to-day performance improvement). He also advises buyers of legal services on legal procurement reviews. Chris's clients include top 20 international law firms as well as FTSE 100 businesses. For ten years he was a director of a UK top 20 law firm where he was head of pricing and conducted innovative research into pricing with Cranfield School of Management. He also has 10 years' consulting experience with PwC, Ernst & Young, and Deloitte. Chris is an international speaker and author on pricing and professional services.

Abigail Hunt is the founder of Abigail Hunt Consulting (www.abigailhunt.com). She works with leading corporate and professional service organisations, helping them to develop new products, services, and strategy, and to build their own internal innovative capacity.

Simon Nash read Law at Bristol University in the UK, and holds the Fellowship of the Chartered Institute of Personnel and Development, and also membership of the British Psychological Society. Until 2017, Simon was the global HR director for Carey Olsen, a prestigious offshore law firm. While at Carey Olsen, he doubled the headcount while the firm tripled financial turnover and achieved Tier One rankings across all practices. Over this time, Simon's people and performance strategy won four major awards and was widely written about in the HR and legal press. Now Simon runs Insight.je, a human factors advisory firm, and ValueMetrix, a business ethics consultancy. He also has interests in two tech start-ups in the HR data analytics space.

J Stephen Poor is chair emeritus of Seyfarth Shaw LLP. He served as chair of the firm from 2001-16, leading the transformation of Seyfarth into an international law firm at the forefront of innovation. In recognition of his work to redefine legal service delivery, Stephen was named the 2011 Legal Innovator of the Year by the *Financial Times*, as well as one of Law360's Most Innovative Managing Partners in 2012. Seyfarth was named "2017 Firm of the Year" by ILTA for its work in robotics.

Scott Rechtschaffen is chief knowledge officer at Littler Mendelson and leads Littler's effort to provide innovative client services by integrating new technologies and work processes and enabling attorneys and clients to access the collective knowledge and experience of the firm's more than 1,000 attorneys. He combines over 25 years of experience representing companies in every area of labor and employment law with a broad understanding of technology to help the firm's attorneys and their clients in tailoring unique solutions that enhance the firm's ability to deliver legal information and legal services to its clients.

Scott heads Littler's knowledge management department comprising dedicated KM attorneys, research specialists, and technologists. He was a member of the multi-disciplinary team that developed the award-winning Littler CaseSmart® approach to legal case management. He oversees the firm's electronic and print publications, internal KMnsystems, and online client subscription services. Scott is the co-founder of ComplianceHR, an innovative joint venture launched by Littler and Neota Logic, a legal software company. ComplianceHR leverages Littler's experience and knowledge of employment law with the power of Neota Logic's expert systems to provide a transformative suite of online compliance solutions for HR and legal professionals. In 2015, the Financial Times presented ComplianceHR with an award for Innovation in The Business of Law: Compliance & Technology.

For his achievements, Scott has been awarded the Distinguished Peer Award as KM Champion of the Year by the International Legal Technology Association, named to the Fastcase 50, an annual compilation "honoring the law's smartest, most courageous innovators", and was named among the 10 most innovative lawyers in North America by the *Financial Times* in 2014.

Kathy Skinner is director of research and information services at White & Case. Kathy's global research and information services team helps lawyers get to the right answers faster. Kathy's responsibilities include delivering an optimal portfolio of research services and products across the firm's 43 offices efficiently and cost-effectively. Kathy's team is part of the broader White & Case knowledge function, led by Oz Benamram.

Deepa Tharmaraj is a legal director for Dell for Middle East and Turkey, a leading consumer and enterprise technology solutions provider. In this role, with senior level experience, she leads legal support for the business, ensuring cost effective and practical legal solutions across different functions and business units. She also serves as the global lead of the "Mosaic" Employee Resource Group at Dell, an organization that is dedicated to increasing awareness and development of culturally intelligent talent, with a focus on community involvement to grow initiatives focused on marginalized communities.

Prior to this role, Deepa was a senior legal counsel at British Telecoms in London and was involved in roles connected to intellectual property, technology transfer and IP product development and procurement. She also supports the Association of Corporate Counsel (GCC chapter) and sits on various judging panels for innovation awards.

Deepa speaks and writes about innovation, including mentoring and encouraging the next generation lawyers, to improve their ability to optimize their innovative attributes. In her free time, she is engaged in various initiatives to mentor and coach the under-privileged.

Chapter 1:
The nature of innovation

By Duncan Hart, barrister

Why is innovation important?

Innovation, to many, is the province of "high tech" companies, particularly those associated with the fast-changing environment of the internet, mobile phone apps, bio-tech, and the like. These are certainly areas where innovation and its impact are most noticeable. In any sector where the fundamental technology underlying the products and services offered is based on microprocessors that double in capacity and halve in cost every 12-18 months[1] this is hardly surprising. Such a rate of change is not only driving innovation, it is opening up new markets, desire for new services, and inspiring new business models.

It's not only the high-tech sector that features strongly in drawing correlations between innovation, profitability, and the sustainability of organisations. The Boston Consulting Group's annual innovation survey[2] has, since 2005 in 15 different market sectors and across 20 countries, made a very strong case for this proposition.

So, how does that perspective influence the apparently less hectic world of the provision of legal and similar services? If technology is arguably not having such an obvious impact, what is the necessity for elevating innovation as a key factor in developing and executing a firm's strategy? What should drive a firm to radically reconsider its mix of services or even its underlying "business model", which describes the building blocks upon which the firm's strategy is built and delivered?

Are their clients being particularly influenced by the winds of change, and are they demanding new ways of engaging with their legal advisors? Can they or should they move to capitalize on those changes and adapt their processes, and re-evaluate the "value" they claim to be delivering to those clients? These are but a few of the drivers behind the current rise in interest in innovation within law firms. So, what leads firms to take this issue more seriously?

The need to take innovation more seriously and to incorporate it into a firm's strategic thinking usually reflects the adoption or recognition of one or more views by a firm's leadership team.[3] Most firms will readily identify many of these influences but struggle to respond in anything other than an "ad hoc" fashion:

- The rate of change in the legal sector is such that innovation is required simply to "stay in the game" and keep up with competitors;
- Regulatory changes are opening up a wide range of alternatives for law firms and non-law firms to compete in the traditional law firm market – the firm feels the need to take advantage of those changes to remain competitive and to lever them to its advantage, as well as to recognize the capacity that such new entrants may have to innovate more quickly and effectively than the present incumbents;
- Clients' needs are changing, and the firm recognizes that innovation is required to satisfy those needs;
- Client demands to require the same services at reduced pricing necessitates innovative solutions be developed by the firm to enable this to be achieved if their services are still to be delivered profitably;
- The firm has or seeks to have the reputation for being "innovative" in all aspects of its practice as this attracts and retains clients;
- "More of the same" doesn't seem to satisfy either staff or clients;
- Innovation attracts and retains "star performers" to the firm who are interested in new ways of practicing law and serving their clients;
- Declining profits demand more than "cost cutting" – the firm needs to invest in developing new services and the capability to develop and deliver them as well as the means to attract premium prices for those services to combat "commoditization";
- To enable the firm to acquire and retain talent, the firm needs to be seen by others in the profession as being capable of demonstrating leadership and innovation in the way in which it manages the changes in the legal market;
- The firm needs to demonstrate improving profitability and new initiatives if it is to satisfy existing and potential stakeholders, whether they be existing employees, investors, or shareholders;
- The firm seems to be steadily going backwards, working ever harder for less profit – something has to change;

- Its major clients are being lost to smaller firms who seem able to not only undercut its prices but offer comparable services and still make a healthy profit;
- Its clients who have been loyal for many years are pointing to initiatives being introduced by other firms and wondering why they are not doing something similar;
- Most of the new technologies that are promoted as being useful in law firms are hardly utilized, or are utilized poorly, and there is no real understanding why or how they can make a difference;
- The firm has seen so many changes in its client base and in the range of services it is being expected to offer in recent years that it needs to view this as "the new normal" and continually invest in the resources and processes required to introduce "innovation" as a permanent feature of its strategy; and
- The firm always seems to be one of the last to respond to emerging needs in its client base – its competitors seem to be able to identify new trends in what clients need, whilst it is always playing "catch-up".

Most firms have experienced some of these concerns from time to time and many have responded, usually in a crisis-driven mode, which may well have produced the necessary changes, some more innovative than others, to deal with the "crisis du jour". In many cases, new leaders are appointed, wholesale changes are made to staff, drastic cost-cutting is introduced, or the firm simply splits and many choose to go their own way. A focus on innovation is not a sure-fire antidote to any of those dramatic outcomes, but it does hold considerable promise for those prepared to make it a central driver in the way in which the firm chooses to do business.

A firm that has stopped or rejects innovation thinking has, in this author's opinion, unwittingly taken the view that they have effectively developed the perfect sustainable strategy and business model, tailored exactly to their client's needs, and which they are confident will never change! What's more, if there are any changes required, they assume they will be given sufficient time to adapt and then business will resume as before with little or no change in profitability.

Such thinking was at best the hallmark of state-controlled and enforced monopolies maintained behind large tariff barriers, or professions where the "barriers to entry" were so high, the terms on which the profession dealt with its clients could practically be dictated by that profession. Neither bears any reasonable resemblance to the dynamism that is evident in today's globalizing capitalist economies and the "de-regulatory" enthusiasm being displayed by most advanced economies.

As Jack Welch of GE fame is reported to have observed, if the rate of change within a company is less than that observed in its customers, then the demise of the company is certain; it's simply a question of time.

In the "legal" business, not only are the clients and markets to which their services are offered under the pressure of fundamental changes, the profession itself no longer enjoys the privileged position and protection it once did.

The choices in my view are fairly clear: unless you happen to hold the view that you have devised the perfect strategy and business model, innovative thinking and action must be a central plank of your firm's strategy. Convulsive and disruptive changes may well occur in any event. Such changes may from time to time be well beyond anyone's control, but we can confidently assume change is and will continue to be required. What's more, it is likely to be of an order and impact far greater than previously experienced as there is considerable evidence that the pace of change driven in particular by so called "transformational" or "platform technologies" is occurring in shorter cycles.

Most firm failures are, however, driven by the impact of more mundane factors associated with an over-dependency on their existing strategies and models, and a refusal or willful neglect to incorporate processes and behaviors to adapt to their changing environment. If that sounds vaguely Darwinian, it is! The critical difference, however, is that unlike most biological cousins we have the ability, foresight, and capability to change other than by waiting for "natural selection" to play its glacial evolutionary role. The question is simply one of whether we are prepared to utilize our faculties to do so. As Peter Theil, one of the founders of PayPal observed, "Darwinism may be a fine theory in other contexts, but in start-ups, intelligent design works best".[4]

What is actually happening that is innovative?

If doubt remains, consider some of the innovations that have attracted attention in recent years in the UK, US, and Australia. Consider for a moment how these innovations may have had an impact. By that I mean how they would have impacted not only critical elements in the firm's business model, such as its cost base, resources, and service offering, but also how clients might have viewed their introduction. Are these innovations merely window dressing? Do they represent a competitive threat to the firms with which these innovators compete? What might they come up with next, and what does the generation and, above all, the implementation of these types of initiatives say about the firm's culture, strategic thinking, and management skills? In markets where competition is intense, in-house counsels are increasingly demanding and innovative in their own right. Do these innovations succeed in differentiating the firms concerned?

It is useful to survey the legal landscape to see what useful examples are already out there. The degree to which any particular initiative is regarded as innovative is not so important perhaps as recognizing that many of today's market leaders are concerned that the traditional legal business model is not necessarily the best means by which they intend to continue to remain competitive. They may not have got it "right" in any game-changing sense, but they are hard at work and in many cases have developed a disciplined process to keep exploring a wide range of options; in the end, this is the only sure way to come up with new solutions.

In a quote attributed to Wim Dejonghe, senior partner of Allen & Overy:

> *"The traditional law firm model is under pressure and you have to decide whether you stick to a diminishing market for 'pure' premium work or accept that to win a greater share of the premium work, you have to combine it with alternative delivery models."*

He also observed that of the 20 top law firms in the UK by revenue, all use a combination of outsourcing, contract lawyers, project management, and technology and process mapping in an attempt to improve cost efficiencies for clients.

Most interestingly, however, the ABS[5] structure in the UK is driving innovation, not only within established legal firms, but in their major clients' business models, in-house counsel, and through private equity investment groups. In Australia, of course, firms are able to go one step further and list on the stock exchange to raise capital. Examples include Shines, Slater & Gordon, and most recently IPH/Sprusons. Listing in late 2014, IPH, a firm with a turnover of approximately A$80 million, raised A$160 million in exchange for approximately half the equity in the company.

The examples discussed below are taken from the Financial Times 2015 Innovative Lawyers report,[6] highlighting the Top 10 game changers of the past 10 years in Europe.

DLA Piper

Pioneer of the Swiss verein structure, under which affiliates remain separate entities, the firm led in showing the profession how to achieve ambitious internationalization without the pain of a full merger. DLA tied up with US law firm Piper Rudnick in 2005 and has since expanded its number of offices from 49 to 88, covering 30 countries. It also led in listening to clients and positioning itself as a business-led law firm.

Latham & Watkins

The firm has built practices in New York and London to rival incumbent leaders. Its growth strategy, commitment to innovation, and effectiveness in lateral hiring have seen it ruffle feathers in key markets, particularly in finance. It has shown that elite firms can build market-leading practices in competitive jurisdictions from scratch.

Axiom

The contracts management business is revolutionizing the way big corporations create and manage commercial contracts. Axiom employs lawyers, project managers, and process engineers who, together with its own technology, provide clients with an alternative to traditional law firms that raises standards for the profession.

Slater & Gordon

The first law firm in the world to float, Slater & Gordon originated in Australia but has gone on to build a significant UK business with the acquisition of nine firms over the past three years. It is changing the way in which consumer law is practiced and how lawyers are perceived in the consumer market.

Allen & Overy

The winner of FT overall law firm innovation awards in four of the past 10 years, Allen & Overy leads the way in showing elite law firms a route to combine premier legal practices with alternative service models such as its online legal services business, aosphere. It bucked the market trend to downsize in the wake of the financial crisis and has increased its number of offices by 92 percent and partner headcount by 100.

Berwin Leighton Paisner

The LOD (Lawyers On Demand) service showed the way for law firms to offer flexible staffing. The scheme has now been copied by 30 percent of the top 20 UK law firms. LOD has grown 700 percent over the past five years. BLP has integrated LOD into a service delivery model.

Eversheds
A series of innovations saw Eversheds enter into the profession's first comprehensive single-supplier relationship with Tyco in 2006, and set up business process engineering in the early 2000s before the disaggregation of legal services was accepted as a market necessity. It set up general counsel initiatives before most law firms saw the importance of the in-house lawyer.

King & Wood Mallesons
The first leading international law firm to be headquartered in the Asia-Pacific region. The tie-up between Chinese law firm King & Wood with Australian firm Mallesons sent waves through the profession and within two years has resulted in a further spate of Anglo-Chinese tie-ups. The subsequent merger with London-based SJ Berwin means it is the first European firm to be able to offer advice from mainland China.

Bird & Bird
The firm grew beyond its boutique roots to become an international player that sticks to the media, technology and life science industries. The focus on industry sectors and related practice areas became a legal profession trend in the late 1990s. Bird & Bird has been doing it for longer and shows how such a strategy pays dividends for a focused law firm.

Garrigues
The firm leads the way on the Iberian peninsula and in Latin America in terms of working differently. It has benefited from the days of its tie-up with Arthur Andersen and is not afraid to experiment with multi-disciplinary teams, technologies and a professional approach to running its partnership. One of the first Iberian firms to publish a social responsibility report in 2006, it continues as an all-equity partnership that regularly occupies the top non-UK European law firm slot in the FT reports.

References

1. Moore's Law.
2. Boston Consulting Group, 'The Most Innovative Companies 2018': www.bcg.com/publications/collections/most-innovative-companies-2018.aspx_
3. This term encompasses formal boards, partnership meetings, managing partners, and any coalition which manages the business and strategic direction of the firm or company.

4. Thiel, P., *Zero to One – Notes on start-ups, or How to build the future*, Crown Books, New York, 2014.
5. Since January 2012 Alternate Business Structures began to be licensed in the UK pursuant to the Legal Services Act 2007.
6. https://ig.ft.com/special-reports/innovative-lawyers/2015/north-america/overall/in-house

Chapter 2:
Disruptive innovation

By Markus Hartung, director at the Bucerius Center on the Legal Profession (CLP) at Bucerius Law School, Hamburg, and Dr Arne Gärtner, senior legal project manager and manager business improvement at Linklaters, Frankfurt

"Consulting on the cusp of disruption" is the title of a widely recognized article about the future of the consulting industry that was published in the October 2013 issue of the *Harvard Business Review*.

The Harvard academics who penned the article (among them the undisputed expert in the field of disruptive innovation, Clayton M Christensen[1]) predicted serious changes – disruption – for the consulting industry. Backing up this prediction, they held up law firms as proof that not even professional services firms are guarded against radical change. Citing many trends that are widely known in the legal industry – the disaggregation of the value chain of traditional law firms, greater use of contract attorneys, the development of new business models and the rise of alternative service providers, and a generally eroding opacity of the law firm business model – the authors plainly showed that, in their eyes, the legal industry was already far from "the cusp of disruption": it was already in the middle of radical change.

The image of the legal industry as a pioneer in the field of disruptive innovation surprised us, since the industry (and especially lawyers) are usually perceived as being rather conservative, and law firms are usually regarded as being the late majority (or even the laggards) when it comes to their rate of adaption to innovation and change. Thinking about this image, we were curious if – on the grounds of our ongoing research on trends in the legal industry – we would find any evidence to prove the thesis presented in the article.

Firstly, we came to the conclusion that our research in the past had focused too much on traditional law firms, legal departments, and their mutual relationship, and not enough on new business models, new services, and alternative providers. The theory of disruptive innovation, however, is based on the belief that new market entrants drive disruptive innovation. Thus, the idea for a new study was born.

Together with The Boston Consulting Group, in 2014 and 2015/2016, we carried out two fundamental studies on the future of the legal industry. In the course of these studies, titled "Trends in the legal market – disruption, evolution or just hype?" and "How Legal Technology Will Change the Business of Law", more than 60 interviews and workshops with legal departments, alternative providers, law firms, and other market experts were carried out. The main goal of the study was to analyze the direction in which the legal market is now headed, and to establish who is in the driver's seat for market developments in the long-run.

In addition, we are constantly conducting extensive literature reviews on the overarching topics of strategy, innovation, trends, and the future of the legal market. This knowledge as well is part of our research and a basis for our findings.

Innovation in the legal market

Before we discuss the details and findings of the study, a brief overview of innovation in the legal market might be helpful for a general understanding of the term "innovation" in this context. "Innovation" means everything that is new and, at the same time, has an economic potential. Being creative and coming up with something new is not sufficient for something to be called "innovative". A lot of what lawyers are doing is highly creative in terms of finding unique solutions to unique problems, but it is not innovative, since these ideas cannot be packaged as "legal products", sold to other clients, or protected under patent or copyright laws. Even if lawyers come up with radically new ideas or products, they cannot protect their ideas.

Every innovation can be categorized in terms of several different dimensions. One dimension is the type of innovation: distinguishing between innovative products, services, processes, or business models. Intensity of innovation is another dimension that makes it possible to distinguish between different kinds of innovation: sustaining, radical, or disruptive.

To lawyers, innovation may have sounded like something strange and new a few years ago. The pre financial crisis legal market was characterized by excess demand. This, combined with two of the main characteristics of the law firm business model (opacity of the delivery model and information asymmetry), made lawyers guarded against innovation and change. Therefore, lawyers didn't need to think about innovation for a long time, and due to the surplus in demand, clients were not in the position to drive innovation and change. That's why lawyers, who are confronted with innovation, especially those from big law firms, usually focused on the question: "why should law firms or legal departments be innovative at all?" As a consequence, they often came up with a number of arguments as to why lawyers and law firms *don't* need to be innovative. But that is the wrong question to ask. The right question is: "why not?"

But for a long time we were discussing a crucial question with lawyers from law firms and legal departments: What makes lawyers so special that they don't need to innovate? Every business in the world needs to innovate in order to gain competitive advantage and survive in the marketplace – and we came to the conclusion that lawyers are no longer an exception to this basic rule. That is why today most of the large law firms and legal departments have institutionalised an innovation program or at least have appointed employees whose job it is to think about how the firm / department can be more innovative. But this alone doesn't necessarily create an environment that automatically leads to disruptive innovation.

Hence, in the course of the study, we were looking for the "conditio sine qua non" of disruptive innovation.

Where does disruption come from?

The theory of disruptive innovation suggests that there are usually new business models or products that disrupt whole markets and, in the end, cast out other (including the leading) market participants – traditional law firms, in our case. That is why we started to analyze different business models and services of various alternative service providers. Further, we examined the value chain and business model of big law firms regarding the question of which elements of the business model alternative providers try to attack and whether this implies any disruptive potential.

Finally, we analyzed the adoption rate of new services and business models from the in-house perspective in order to analyze the market penetration of alternative providers. The role and importance of alternative services providers had to be looked at in more detail than before. We therefore came to the conclusion that we are on the verge of a new legal ecosystem, which now has three groups of market participants.

Alternative providers: A broad range of different firms

Today, alternative service providers are broadly described as market participants with non-traditional (including non-lawyer) business models. This definition is imprecise, almost meaningless. What is "traditional" in this regard? The traditional law firm business model is normally referred to as a partnership with the classical pyramid model and a leverage structure. Non-traditional or alternative (as in an alternative to the traditional law firm) providers, on the other hand, are often organized as corporations, rather than partnerships, and are oriented around fundamentally different rules and goals. There are alternative business models that have existed for a long time now, but equally there are new business models that have only been developed in recent years.

Our research found, accordingly, that the lack of a distinction between categories of alternative service providers made it impossible to form a general statement as to whether they might disrupt the legal industry. The business models and innovative ideas of the various alternative providers are simply too fundamentally different. That is why our study – for the first time – classified alternative service providers into different categories, based on their business models and the services they offer. We found a total of eight different types of alternative providers. But before we go into this, a health warning is required: These findings stem from 2013/2014. Since then, the market has dramatically changed, hence the following categories are not completely up to date (but by no means completely out of date!)

Classification of alternative providers

The longest-established and best-known alternative providers are insourcing/lawyers on demand firms and legal process outsourcing (LPO) firms that mostly deliver standardized and partly automated tasks in the fields of due diligence or e-discovery. These are the most successful models in terms of market penetration and size of firm. In addition to LPO and insourcing firms, we identified six other types of alternative providers. There are a number of providers already active in all of these areas. The categories can be described as follows:

1. Legal process outsourcing (LPO) firms provide low-cost work with low complexity/criticality. Firms include Pangea3, Axiom, or CPA Global.
2. Insourcing firms offer temporary legal staffing services to cover peaks or gaps at legal departments and law firms. Examples are Axiom, Lawyers On Demand, or Eversheds Agile.
3. Providers of complex projects/managed legal services include, on the one hand, big management consultant and audit firms like

BCG, McKinsey, PwC, EY, or Deloitte, and on the other hand firms like Axiom, Radiant Law, or Riverview Law. They provide services for the management of more complex/critical projects, often with extended responsibilities.

4. Alternative/virtual law firms provide traditional legal advice services, but without the typical overhead costs and often on a fixed-fee basis. The lawyers are virtually connected. Virtual law firms included Clearspire (which was still going at the time of the study) and gunnercooke.
5. Self-service platforms are tailored platforms for legal needs and questions. They offer both legal document generation services, as well as supplementary legal advice and Q&A.
6. Online resolution platforms are self-service platforms as well. The most prominent example is Modria.
7. Providers of research and information services offer customized legal research on demand. Their research is based on databases and libraries. Firms offering research and information services include Thomson Reuters and Lois Law.
8. Quantitative legal analytics providers offer high-end statistical products, for instance statistics to predict law suit outcomes or IT-based management of billings. Examples are TyMetrics, Lawyer Metrics, and Lex Machina.
9. Networking platforms are structured to enable the exchange of legal information, e.g. collaboration systems for in-house counsel in the form of closed communities. See, for example, Legal OnRamp or Advance Law.
10. Artificial Intelligence (AI) providers that make especially ediscovery or due diligence processes more efficient, examples include Kira, RAVN or Casepoint.

All of the firms listed above have entered the marketplace with innovative ideas and business models. But it is still an open question whether these firms have the potential to disrupt the legal industry. To answer this question, it is important to analyze each firm's "point of attack".

Point of attack: The value chain of law firms

Alternative business models try to exploit at least one shortcoming of traditional law firms. Three of the most common weaknesses of law firms are:

(i) Lack of sufficient IT – in terms of collaboration and knowledge management systems;

(ii) Lack of project management skills – in terms of management of complex projects where legal is only one part of a bigger picture; and

(iii) Lack of efficiency – in terms of high costs and poor processes. Therefore, the business models of alternative providers are usually IT-driven, efficiency-driven, or project management-driven.

Some of the providers strive in more than one direction. But the value chain of traditional law firms can be further differentiated between primary and secondary or support activities.

Although there is no common or unanimous view on primary and secondary activities, we would argue that primary activities are in general resources planning, project management, information gathering, legal research, negotiation, and contract drafting. Secondary activities are supportive of law firm infrastructure, human resources management, procurement, business development, innovation, and strategy.

Regarding primary activities, most of the above-described models only offer services that change a part of the value chain of traditional law firms. Lawyers On Demand, for example, aim to offer better options for resources planning, but no legal services. Or consider LPO: they deal with simple, and often standardized, tasks – e.g. electronic discovery, information gathering, due diligence services – but they don't offer legal advice. And then there are firms that offer legal information and research services, aiming to offer better value for money to law firms and legal departments. Thus, seven of these categories mainly offer specialized, niche products and don't really compete with traditional law firms. They offer services that might replace parts of the value chain of law firms, but they cannot replace law firms entirely. That doesn't mean that these firms cannot be profitable; on the contrary, the specialization might lead to a very good market position with good margins. Firms specializing in only a small part of the value chain can be very successful, but we assume that they cannot foster radical change and disruption. Only virtual law firms and providers of managed legal services, partly offering the same services as traditional law firms, try to supersede traditional law firms in large part, and thus might carry the potential to replace some services law firms are offering.

At the present time, alternative providers are mainly focused on standardized or automated tasks, and on particular parts of the law firm value chain, where a sophisticated IT structure and efficient processes are regarded as a competitive advantage. More and more companies are sending the more standardized or automated tasks to alternative providers, or are convincing their law firms of choice to outsource such work or leverage distinctive technologies, such as AI when it comes to due diligence, to decrease costs. But when it comes to medium and high-end tasks, law firms are still the natural choice. For now. There are already alternative providers striving to move up the value chain, and more and more are competing directly with law firms.

Who drives innovation and change

Irrespective of the actual market penetration of alternative providers, the existence of new providers with innovative business models is undoubtedly a growing phenomenon. The existence of innovative ideas, new business or delivery models, and alternative providers is perhaps a necessary condition for innovation and radical change in the legal market, but it is hardly a sufficient cause.

What really drives innovation and change is the necessity or the sheer pressure to be innovative. Being innovative is not a "lifestyle decision". Only companies that are ultimately paying the bills of both law firms and alternative providers need to find innovative ways to deliver legal services. Hence, there is a pressure on general counsel to find new ways to deliver legal services to the company. Mostly this pressure comes directly from the CFO or the CEO.

Legal departments are under pressure to fundamentally change the way in which they deliver legal services to their company; hence, they will increasingly pile the pressure both on law firms and alternative providers to deliver added value and to come up with radically different ways to deliver legal services. General counsel are in the driver's seat when it comes to future developments in the legal industry, and they will determine the direction in which the market is headed, and ultimately the future of both law firms and alternative providers. Without a direct, identifiable benefit for the companies involved, the good ideas behind every major innovation will remain no more than that: ideas.

Core hypotheses derived from the study

In the course of the study, we developed some overall hypotheses on the future of the legal market in general, and on the future of the three market participants. The legal market is currently in a flux and significant changes are starting to happen. Alternative providers are something new to the legal market and they are absolutely here to stay. But they need to prove their added value over a long period of time to really become a serious threat to law firms (as true competitors) and legal departments (as a real alternative to traditional law firms).

At the same time, some law firms have fully realized that alternative / technology providers can only take away market share from them as ´long as they aren't working efficiently. Therefore these firms are spending time and resources to understand their value chains and come up with ideas to produce their services at a lower cost. Therefore these firms will be in a better position regarding the overall competitive situation in the market.

The most important driver for change for now is IT: what can be done through IT and software will be done through IT and software (even if quality levels are slightly lower). This opens up room for alternative providers, as traditional law firms often lack the required knowledge and energy when it comes to accomplishing tasks in the most efficient way.

The question of disruption is of second order – it is a (slow) evolutionary development towards a more nuanced landscape of different legal providers, meeting more specifically articulated client needs. Legal departments need time to adjust to the new provider landscape; hence, only alternative providers who pursue a long-term strategy will succeed in the long-run. General counsel will continue to profoundly test and question every new service or business model to establish if it can really add value.

Hence, more innovative delivery models that were very recently initiated are of course interesting, but the broad market proof of concept is still pending. Long-established alternative providers are increasingly and successfully becoming integrated into the market – particularly the insourcing market segment has turned out to be a very profitable (niche) market. Simultaneously, alternative providers are trying to move up the value chain ("managed legal services") and succeed in the first lighthouse projects. The use of alternative providers should not be overrated, however; developing a brand is a long-haul exercise, a marathon rather than a sprint, and law firms will only be partially threatened by alternative providers. High-end legal advice remains the home turf of big law, but low/medium work and second/third tier law firms will be severely impacted. Law firms, not known as disruptors themselves, should more actively embrace the opportunities this new environment offers – even considering to acquire an alternative provider. Be that as it may, most law firms still enjoy the extremely powerful position as the first point of call when it comes to legal or regulatory issues. They should leverage this hallowed position as long as they have the opportunity to do so: for as long as it takes alternative service providers to develop a similar position of strength.

Reference

1. Clayton M Christensen introduced the term "disruptive technologies" in 1995, and has written several books on disruptive innovation. He is widely recognised as the expert in this field.

Chapter 3: Why creativity and innovation are the key to value enhancement for legal departments

By Deepa Tharmaraj, legal director at Dell Middle East, Africa & Turkey

This chapter considers how in-house counsels' value enhancement strategies can positively influence the growth strategies of law firms, by providing insights into a legal department's innovative solutions and their drivers for creativity and innovation. The chapter describes creativity and innovation from a legal counsel's perspective – in an in-house legal department – but these principles can be applied to lawyers in general.[1]

Drivers of a changing market from the client's perspective

There are five things that every law firm needs to know about its clients; often clients tell the firm two or three of these things, but not all five. Understanding their clients' needs will reveal that general counsel in legal departments have the same pressures as their businesses do, and the same pressures as the law firms do: keeping the cost down and meeting the key performance indicators such as value-added services, operational excellence, and client satisfaction.

Law firms recognize that their clients, as buyers, are innovating to extract best value from their vendors and are testing out new procurement practices to identify new sources of service providers. The question is, what makes a law firm stand out in the eyes of this generation of legal service buyers? Do law firms understand that legal departments have to change and that, unless they change, they will not survive in their current shape? Naturally, these changes permeate through their relationships with outside counsel, and may shed light on why in-house counsel are demanding change from the law firms they appoint.

Law firms need to accept that they are pivotal to the success of the legal department and its business. Before exploring this, I want to share the five things that every law firm needs to know about the legal departments it works with:

1. Legal departments are prioritizing simplification, standardization, and automation of routine work and templates of contracts and letters;
2. Legal counsel invest time and effort in building long term and open relationships, based on trust, with their outside counsel;
3. In-house lawyer and outside counsel engagement increases where the parties are co-creating innovative solutions collaboratively, and sharing the pain and gain of these innovative solutions;
4. Legal counsel expect accurate and precise advice from their outside counsel – there is very little room for error or doubt; and
5. Legal counsel want to see their outside counsel driving value creation, and translating that to value-added services for the legal department as a natural by-product of the relationship.

With the democratization of legal services, legal counsel are increasingly relying on the existing tools and resources within their organization in order to innovate and are refusing to pay extra money for things that they can do themselves. However, it is fair to say that not all legal counsel apply innovative thinking. Could the resistance to innovate stem from legal training?

In-house lawyers have multi-disciplinary stakeholders, and businesses' expectations of in-house legal departments are changing considerably. The business and its legal counsel are interdependent; however, that interdependency has to be balanced with the independence required of a legal counsel who has to prioritize the role of risk manager. Our job is to connect the business, support functions and operations, and to ensure compliance at all levels. Business needs and regulatory requirements are changing rapidly and therefore the speed at which we have to respond to those needs is increasing dramatically, primarily due to the technology that is available today. With these demands from the business and a regulated environment, both law firms and legal counsel need the agility and zeal of a start-up to develop innovative ideas which will enable and empower the general counsel to meet the legal department's KPIs.

This chapter is divided loosely into three main themes:

1. Culture to innovate;
2. Opportunities to innovate; and
3. Tools for innovation.

There is a plethora of research and literature on the first two sections in legal publications, and materials on change management and culture, and those interested in reading further on this subject should look to the several esteemed publications and authors cited at the end of this chapter. I will also discuss tools for innovation – because these are tools that are not specifically designed for legal practitioners. Years of working with researchers and engineers had aroused my curiosity to search for ways to innovate in my legal role, and I describe some of these in this chapter.

As for the law firms, this chapter is an opportunity to see things from our perspective and how we are developing innovative ideas to meet our client needs and KPIs.

Creativity and innovation

> *"If we never do anything which has not been done before, we shall never get anywhere. The law will stand still while the rest of the world goes on, and that will be bad for both."*
>
> Lord Denning, *Packer v. Packer* (1954)

Before I proceed, we need to be on the same page about the definitions of creativity and innovation. "Creativity is the capability or act of conceiving something original or unusual. Innovation is the implementation of something new"[2] because innovation is the ability to apply a new approach to a fundamental problem which could result in an incremental or a breakthrough benefit.

I think the rigorous law training during the undergraduate or pre-law program, and the subsequent Bar and law school, develops abstract thinking, problem solving, and analytical skills, especially through the countless hours of cramming case law and codified statutes – and not to mention all the Latin words! I am convinced that the demanding law training has prepared us for the highest order of thinking skills. Bloom's Taxonomy was developed by Benjamin Bloom to set out six classifications of thinking corresponding to cognitive levels of complexity.[3] The six classifications are remembering, understanding, applying, analyzing, evaluation, and creation. Creation! Since creation involves something new and possibly useful, I believe that our legal training has equipped us to be creative and innovative; but we often stop before we embark on the next step. The central tenet of this chapter is to highlight the importance of embracing the culture of innovation in legal departments, and look at examples of the types of opportunities that are available to legal counsel working in small or large in-house legal departments, whether in headquarters or regional offices.

Culture to innovate

> *"To truly experience living and not merely existing throughout our (legal) careers, business and life, the progressive evolutionary dynamics of our present decade (and beyond for that matter) is compelling us to get out of our comfort zones, to dare to be different, and ultimately to re-invent ourselves."*
>
> Chrissie Lightfoot, *Tomorrow's Naked Lawyer*

Many legal departments today are experimenting with new business models, process improvements, and technology-led systems and tools to extract value and cost savings in response to the incredible pressures they are facing from their cost centers. The challenges and the problems we face could be bucketized roughly into the triangle of people, process, and technology. We could connect innovative ideas to one of the three pillars, which represent a rudimentary framework for the purposes of this chapter, and each pillar if explored in conjunction with the tools of innovation could produce some powerful and innovative results.

People

Innovation starts with an individual who has an idea, and the motivation to develop the idea to solve a problem. But the motivation has to drive the initiative to obtain stakeholders' buy-in, build a prototype of the idea, test the idea, implement change management, and finally share the end product with other team members. This may work in an ideal world, but the challenge is that every one of the described steps involves the availability of time and collaboration with colleagues and peers on the part of the individual lawyer. In reality, turning a kernel of an idea into full-blown innovation and solution is a monumental quest.

So the question we always ask is: why does one company's in-house department get its act together and produce innovative results in a sustainable manner, while another company of a comparable status does not? Does the answer lie with the leadership?

A leader in an in-house legal department, who promotes and encourages original ideas and process improvements and embraces technology to modernize the legal department and its people, will make innovation happen. A leader who engages their people to think innovatively and work collaboratively across teams, lines of business, and support functions (e.g. finance, tax, and HR) will foster innovation. A step further: successful innovative environments accept failure as an essential ingredient to innovation. Failures or mistakes do not have to be celebrated, but should be investigated to explore the reason for the unsuccessful innovation. When we collaborate, we bring different perspectives and flavors of interpretation to the problem. Unless the different perspectives are managed in a cohesive manner in a team environment, the ideas and perspectives could create awkwardness or a hostile environment. In *Collective Genius*,[4] the concept of "creative abrasion" has been used to reinforce the theory that innovative solutions emerge from "a series of sparks, not from a single flash of insight, as group members play off one another, each member's contribution inspiring the next." So constructive feedback and powerful criticism, when applied properly, can be "an engine of innovation".[5]

Vineet Nayar of HCL Technologies said in *Collective Genius* that innovative leaders are "social architects"; collective result outstrips individual effort when the team is led by a leader who prioritizes innovation in every aspect – time, resources, and money.

Process

The one constant that charts across every part of an organization is process. An end-to-end process in a framework aims to capture a holistic view of internal control systems to manage, produce, or deliver something. It delineates dependencies and inter-dependencies between lines of business or functions; if the process is robust and is complied with, we grow in efficiency and competitiveness. Process can also stifle innovation if it is applied and approached in a rigid manner. But with the innovation trend bucking up, we are starting to recognize process innovation resulting in process improvements.

Replacing a manual process for work intake and allocation to a team of lawyers with an automated system of self-triage questions and answers, culminating with a web-based intake process, is an innovation that in-house legal departments have deployed successfully, and is becoming popular as a way of cutting costs and increasing productivity. One such example is found at British Telecom. BT general counsel Chris Fowler explains:

"All requests for legal work within GS [BT's Global Services] come in through a web-based system and go directly to UnitedLex, which evaluates the request based on complexity; more complex tasks are passed to the in-house legal team in the UK while low-value, high-volume, repeatable tasks stay with UnitedLex".[6]

Technology

Technology is integral to a discussion about innovation and creativity; it has become ubiquitous and plays an integral role in every aspect of an individual's life. The founder and CEO of Dell Inc, Michael Dell, famously said: "Technology is about enabling human potential". We cannot underestimate the power of technology and its usefulness in the innovation ecosystem.

One of the key areas that in-house legal counsel focus on in order to reduce the reactive work is to deliver regular training to clients on different topics – for example, boilerplate terms on customer and distribution contracts, playbooks, policies, operational processes, tools, and self-help flowcharts and wizards.

The training and the transfer of knowledge – and accountability – from the legal team to the sales teams and support functions will transform these individuals into legal and compliance evangelists. As evangelists, they will educate their peers, customers, vendors, and partners to operate within the legal parameters set out in the documents listed above.

When it comes to delivering that training, what choices do we have as in-house counsel when there is a huge training need across the country or regions? We could deliver face-to-face training, which would require money and time. An alternative is online training delivered through e-learning platforms, videos, podcasts, or mobile applications. The latter requires time and money too, but the fact that it is created for repeated use, for audiences locally and globally, makes the return on investment a compelling business case while at the same time it enables us to monitor the attendance and completion of the training programs.

Opportunities to innovate

> *"Still, there is no escaping the fact that there is more to do with less time, less money and fewer people."*
>
> Richard G Stock, Inside Counsel

Utilizing resources

Legal counsel have certain resources to maximize our competency as effective lawyers. These include administrative and paralegal support, data analysts, investigators, translators, and more or less generous budgets for IT and outside counsel spend. The question is whether limited resources translate to limited innovation. An interesting perspective on this issue can be found in a book entitled *Jugaad Innovation*,[7] in which the authors have approached innovation from a frugal perspective in the face of resource constraints. As long as we have the culture of innovation, we can charge ahead to do things in a new way through the "do-it-yourself" method: cheap, quick, and simple innovation.

To enable us to discharge fully our responsibilities we must be prepared to be innovative in our day-to-day work, which will free up our time to attend to the areas that pose the highest risk in other parts of the business. Being proactive and undertaking preventative work requires time for reflection, and if we are busy being reactive we may "lose sight of the shore". As general legal counsel, the neglect of the proactive part of our role could warp our professional outlook and career development. As the saying goes, "necessity is the mother of all invention" – since we understand the problem or the challenge, we can apply a new vision or perspective to a fundamental problem that improves on processes, technology, or costs. If we are sitting at the decision- making table of the business leaders, business typically welcomes cutting-edge ideas from legal to ensure that risks are mitigated and it is legally compliant when products are sold into new markets, while still keeping the cost down.

Legal counsel have opportunities to innovate even when there are limited means to apply creativity. For example, in the application of the strict interpretation of the law in a given situation, legal advice could be communicated to clients in a creative manner. There are references to legal departments using social media, whether internal platforms such as Salesforce.com or external platforms like Facebook and Twitter, to communicate legal updates to their masses of employees and contractors in a bid to reduce email churn.[8] These bursts of legal updates in bite-sized chunks capture the attention of the busy audience of sales makers and employees at large because they are delivered in a short and targeted way. The power of social media in communicating in a one-to-many forum is effective.

Innovation to drive value

Furthermore, we have to manage the outside counsel budgets and build relationships with the outside counsel. Law schools have not trained us to operate businesses and become commercially savvy; neither is an MBA a necessary prerequisite to be a general legal counsel. However, we need to find ways to become better at controlling outside counsel costs. Law firms have begun to offer capped fees, value-based fees, fixed fees, success-based fees, and other alternatives to the billable hour for specific matters. Sometimes, law firms are open to a hybrid model in which a percentage of the fee is based on the hourly rate and the rest is contingent on the outcome of the matter.

As legal counsel, we must be willing to innovate and to care about driving the most competitive rates for a specific matter. Negotiating an alternative fee arrangement (AFA) may create a sense of vulnerability because AFAs are still not commonplace within many of the top-tier firms today, but it starts with one small step from the legal counsel – willingness to innovate.

As fundamental as it is to managing the external spend with our outside counsel, innovation can be found in other parts of the relationship with the law firm. In the following paragraphs we will see how innovation can be applied in areas other than costs:

1. Alternatives to the request for proposal (RFP) process for selection of law firms; and
2. Access to previously issued legal advice.

Alternatives to the RFP process

When reduction of outside counsel fees is the tone set from the top in in-house legal departments, legal counsel who procure legal services for their organizations use RFPs to drive better pricing from the bidding law firms. The whole process starts with issuing the RFP, then evaluating the responses, and selecting the law firm. Nothing in this process involves the technical assessment of the law firm and its lawyers. The question-and-answer sessions and customer testimonials will give us an insight into the capability of the firm and its priorities, but it is not enough to test it on its competency. We could gauge its competency by giving the firm some paid work to assess the quality of its technical knowledge, speed of response, and so on, and measure other metrics that we would use to score the response.

Are your clients considering replacing or supplementing the traditional RFP process? At Dell, we asked the firms that aspired to provide legal services to our company in one country to spend two to three days in our local office on a non-paid basis to assess key risk areas in our local business. After a series of interviews with key functions, such as HR, marketing, and trade, each firm produced a report setting out its views on key risk areas, and recommendations. The report gave us a clear picture of the law firms' competency and capability from different angles – the depth of technical knowledge, pragmatism in the advice, and many other relevant areas. At this point, we had insight into their technical skills from a practical perspective and we could focus on the remainder of the RFP process, which was to apply the scorecard metrics to the other parts of the procurement of legal services exercise, such as value-added services, fees, and international presence. Needless to say, the reports themselves were great resources!

Access to previously issued legal advice

One of the first tasks of an incoming in-house counsel taking over from a predecessor will be to gain access to all the previously issued advice from outside counsel. Unless the organization has a document management system that stores outside counsel advice, the incoming counsel will tend to rely on their predecessor to forward the historical advice; this is the case at Dell. This, of course, assumes that the outgoing lawyer had a management system to store the advice and backed up that advice. As long as we exercise caution, the previously issued advice is a valuable resource to reduce the duplication of instruction to outside counsel.

Alternatively, the bigger law firms are now starting to offer web-based portals that store all of the historical legal opinions and advice. It is an excellent inter-organizational bridge because it provides access to the advice not only to the incoming legal counsel, but also to all other lawyers within the organization.[9]

This reduces cycle time as we have easy access to historical advice, and it helps us control our costs with outside counsel. Both of these innovation examples target the controlling of outside counsel spend, doing more with less, optimizing the resources of the organization without weakening our legal role or our duty to our internal clients, and building our relationships with our outside counsel through innovative approaches.

Tools for innovation

"Genius is one percent inspiration, and ninety-nine percent perspiration."

Thomas Edison

Have you ever wondered how we can stimulate innovative ideas? Unless a light bulb moment occurs or periods of reflection give rise to an idea, generating that idea is no easy feat. Some help is needed!

In a previous publication I have considered the notion that, as in-house counsel, we can learn from others who have gone before us in different industries, business functions, or international standard bodies, as the information is widely available on the internet.[10] There are plenty of toolkits that provide guidance on ways in which we can produce innovative ideas that deliver efficiency and cost savings. Most of us have tried one or more of the following methodologies: brainstorming; Six Sigma[11] for

Lean law; the Kaizen approach to eliminate waste; fishbone cause-and-effect diagram; the affinity diagram; or, most recently, crowdsourcing.

In fact, in Dell, the legal innovation team organized a global legal hackathon – similar to the UK's Dragon's Den TV show for aspiring entrepreneurs – across its four global regional legal teams to stir the creative streaks in the team members.

The result was about 30 innovative solutions for various problem statements. The fishbone cause-and-effect diagram is a powerful tool for problem-solving, too, in a team environment. The team will define the problem statement, and identify all the contributing causes of the problem. Once the causes are identified, they will conduct a root cause analysis to establish what is causing each issue and take steps to eliminate it.

Another positive by-product of this problem-solving approach is that engaging team members in developing the solution automatically increases the buy-in to the changes which have to be implemented.

One toolkit that legal departments have rarely discussed is TRIZ.[12] Engineers and research scientists in the technology and manufacturing sector use TRIZ principles as a creative problem-solving technique; TRIZ is derived from the study of patterns in past inventions and patents. Karen Gadd, in her book *TRIZ for Engineers: Enabling Inventive Problem Solving*,[13] explains the TRIZ methodology as a toolkit to guide engineers to understand their problem, articulate their ideal outcome, and then, by using data, logic, and research within TRIZ, develop an innovative solution. While TRIZ may not have been used widely by lawyers, Lilly Haines-Gadd says:

"TRIZ is an attempt to try to cut across different disciplines and 'bottle' the fundamental logic of problem solving for everyone no matter what their job, specialty or area of expertise."[14] In-house counsel have hope!

We can use TRIZ-based problem solving capabilities to develop innovative ideas. TRIZ has a number of toolkits and each one is suitable for a particular type of situation or problem.

One of my favorites is "40 principles"; it means there are 40 different ways of solving a physical or technical contradiction. A physical contradiction exists when we want opposite solutions. An example of physical contradiction is that training our sales teams comprehensively would take a long preparation time, but we want to deliver it in the minimum time. A technical contradiction is where we improve something, but the improvement also attracts something negative. An example of a technical contradiction in our industry is training – training our clients reduces compliance risks (good), but keeps our sales makers away from selling (bad).[15]

The advantage with the 40 inventive principles is that we can use the principles to eliminate contradictions in a solution – there is no need to choose between the good and bad solution; we can have both opposites or the improvement and the negative as a good solution. But first we have to understand the problem and define the ideal outcome. The common inventive principles are:

- Segmentation – for example, an intake process for allocation of work to a different category of legal team members;
- Self-service – for example, an automated triage on the web with questions and answers for frequently asked questions; and
- The other way around – for example, instead of a legal department storing its outside counsel advice, the outside counsel could provide access rights to a web-based database containing the advice, stored in a structured and systematic arrangement.

The Oxford Creativity TRIZ principles present a clear problem-solving technique. This includes:

- defining the ideal outcome and seeking ideas for ideal solutions;
- identifying, and seeking available resources to provide, the main functions of those ideal solutions; and
- using the inventive principles to eliminate any contradictions in order to produce an innovative idea that can be put into production.

One of the 40 inventive principles is to copy – for example, the in-house counsel can copy the engineer's ways of developing an invention using the TRIZ methods.

Some of the ideas that have been implemented in legal departments – such as automation of templates, standardization of routine work, automation of self-triage using decision trees, e-learning and interactive training, dynamic heat maps, contract generators, and mobile applications – are good examples of innovation and I would not be surprised if each of them was a TRIZ-inspired creation!

Conclusion

"I think that's the single best piece of advice: constantly think about how you could be doing things better, and questioning yourself."

Elon Musk, CEO of Tesla

Pressures on cost savings, advances in technology, and access to top talent from all different parts of the world have justified embracing innovation and creativity as a way to run lean legal departments, while maintaining maximum compliance in the business. In this chapter we have looked at several ways in which in-house legal departments can promote and foster innovation, through the combined forces of forward-thinking leadership and a change in culture and the mindsets of the legal team members. For both in-house and outside counsel, innovation and creativity starts in law school; poring over the law books, case law, and statutes, and understanding their application to the exam questions, requires some problem solving skills – albeit basic skills. The structures of the law curriculum provide a good foundation on which to develop complex problem-solving skills; however, unless we are motivated and curious to ask "why", "what", and "how" when faced with a problem, and then do something about it, innovation will simply be a buzzword. In-house legal departments have proven to be as successful as law firms in developing innovative business models that benefit their clients. A business's success hinges upon its ability to innovate and willingness to innovate; the same expectation applies to its legal department. Law firms' partnership with legal departments will drive a shared success in innovation in the legal industry as a whole.

References

1. This chapter is written based on my experiences and does not represent the views of my employer, Dell, except where I have cited Dell.
2. Sloane, P., "What is the difference between innovation and creativity?", www.innovationexcellence.com, 7 June 2010. See www.innovationexcellence.com/blog/2010/06/07/what-is-the-difference-between-innovation-and-creativity/.
3. Bloom, B. S.; Engelhart, M. D.; Furst, E. J.; Hill, W. H.; Krathwohl, D. R., *Taxonomy of Educational Objectives: The Classification of Educational Goals. Handbook I: Cognitive Domain*. New York: David McKay Company, 1956.
4. Hill, L. A., Brandeau, G., Truelove, E. and Lineback, K., *Collective Genius: The Art and Practice of Creating Innovation*, Boston: Harvard Business School Publishing, 2014.
5. Verganti, R., "The innovative power of criticism", *Harvard Business Review*, Jan-Feb 2016.
6. Chris Fowler, General Counsel, UK, British Telecom, www.acc.com/valuechallenge/valuechamps/2013champ_profilebt.cfm.
7. Radjou, N., Prabhu, J. and Ahuja, S., Jugaad: *Innovation: Think Frugal, Be Flexible, Generate Breakthrough Growth*, California: Jossey-Bass, 2012.
8. Example of micro-blogging and instant messaging by China State Construction, 2013 ACC Value Champion:

https://www.acc.com/valuechallenge/valuechamps/2013champ_profilechinastate.cfm.

9. In some countries, the concept of legal and litigation privilege and attorney-client privilege may prevent open access of certain advice to legal counsel outside the country it was issued from. Please exercise with caution. In the *Harvard Business Review* article "Meeting the challenge of disruptive change" (March-April 2000), Clayton M. Christensen and Michael Overdorf have added that in addition to resources and process, the company's values affect what an organization can and cannot do for disruptive innovation.
10. www.theoath-me.com/s/in-house-view-embracing-innovation.
11. A renowned author who speaks and writes regularly on this topic is Ken Grady, who is the Lean Law Evangelist for Seyfarth Shaw LLP.
12. Russian acronym for the "theory of inventive problem solving" developed by G. S. Altshuller and his colleagues in the former USSR between 1946 and 1985.
13. Gadd, K., *TRIZ for Engineers: Enabling Inventive Problem Solving*, Sussex: John Wiley & Sons, 2011.
14. Haines-Gadd, L., *TRIZ for Dummies*, Chichester: John Wiley & Sons, 2016.
15. See www.mindtools.com/pages/article/newCT_92.htm.

Chapter 4:
Building a culture of innovation in legal services

By Adam Billing, partner, and Abigail Hunt, associate, at Møller PSF Group

The innovation imperative

The trends that are driving change in the legal sector are well known: clients demanding more for less, the billable hour under fire, shifting workforce demographics, the growing need for global reach. These trends are all exacerbated by new technologies that enable, among other things, greater legal process outsourcing, e-discovery, and virtual working. All of these factors, combined with new client needs and regulatory changes, create an environment ripe for disruption in terms of how legal services are delivered, what those services might include, as well as who is delivering them.

At the present time, the greatest impetus for change in legal services is coming from in-house legal teams. These teams are under pressure to deliver both more and different strategic value to their own changing businesses.

Des Woods, chairman and a founding partner of the Møller PSF Group at Cambridge University, said:

"Clients complain constantly that their legal suppliers are behind the game in terms of innovating around service delivery and pricing. Their view is that most innovation is in the in-house lawyer community, as they face direct budget pressure from their boards. Having said that, the market has definitely woken up and many, but not all, firm leaders are gearing up for major change."

How long will it take to reach a tipping point when some law firms will be forced to change their model? And how long before innovation is at the top of the agenda for more than just the most forward-looking firms?

Greg Bott, head of the Client Development Centre for Addleshaw Goddard LLP, commented:

"The improving economy might have been detrimental to the rise of innovation – hiding some of the issues and cracks. A slight cooling may help unearth those things that need to be addressed."

Exactly how the legal services landscape will evolve over the coming years is far from certain. What is definite, however, is that innovation will play a central role in this evolution.

A culture of innovation

With some notable exceptions, much of the innovation that has taken place in the legal sector has been what can be described as "spot innovation". These are innovations that occur in response to a particular client request, regulatory change, or internal business challenge – not the result of a strategic and coordinated effort to drive growth and profitability through innovation.

Legal sector innovation

Over the last few years, legal sector innovation has received increasing attention in the media and from a growing number of awards bodies. New service, product, strategy, and process innovations have in many cases been driven by advances in technology that are transforming the way work is managed and delivered, both externally and internally.

While these successes should not be undervalued, innovation in legal services is still rarely taking place at the level required to take full advantage of the opportunities ahead and to cope with the magnitude of change and uncertainty building within the sector. This requires a more systemic and intentional approach than currently exists in most firms today. It requires a "culture of innovation".

In recent years, "creating a culture of innovation" has become a frequently cited strategic objective for businesses of all kinds. But what does that really mean?

We define a culture of innovation as the collective practices, mindsets, policies, and norms that enable an organization to make innovation part of business as usual. In this type of culture, innovation is a core, constant activity of the organization – as opposed to something that is done in addition to the "real" work of the firm.

When a culture of innovation is in place, the firm is inherently better able to identify new opportunities as they emerge, think creatively about how to respond, and mobilize resources to rapidly develop and implement solutions. Specifically, this results in:

- Greater agility and responsiveness to change;
- Improved collaboration across the firm, with clients and other parties;
- Profitable new revenue streams and internal cost savings;
- Improved employee engagement and productivity; and
- Increased growth potential and competitive advantage.

How this manifests will vary widely from firm to firm. There is no one-size-fits-all solution – nor are there transferrable templates to follow. Organizational strategy, structure, history, and innovation objectives all have a profound effect on the shape a firm's culture of innovation needs to take to be effective.

However, from our experience of working in the professional services and corporate sectors, a number of lessons learned and key success factors have emerged that can help law firms create an innovation culture that produces the desired results, while avoiding some of the most common pitfalls.

Legal sector innovation in action: External strategies

Externally focused innovations include new legal strategies, such as Simmons & Simmons' creation of a cost and time saving strategy to redirect PPI litigation away from the courts, and instead into its clients' internal complaint-handling functions. Or novel service offerings, such as Hogan Lovells' creation of the Privacy Innovation Assessment, a tool that helps clients assess the privacy implications of new business developments and recommends practical steps to address them.

Legal sector innovation in action: Alternative service providers

AdventBalance, a young Australian firm offering fixed rates, lawyer pools, and a unique staffing arrangement, whereby top-tier experienced lawyers work directly in client businesses on a secondment basis, has enjoyed double and even triple digit growth rates in the last five years. Schillings reorganized itself entirely when it moved to ABS status and repositioned itself as a multi-disciplinary firm offering a comprehensive reputation defense package made up of consultancy services, cyber security services, and legal assistance. Since the change, the firm's revenue has climbed by 30 percent.

Create the foundation – Building skills and awareness

The bedrock of a strong innovation culture is a shared understanding of how innovation works and the business case for doing it. This requires a common framework that everyone can easily grasp, apply, and practice – forming the basis for a common language and approach for how innovation happens in the firm. Creating this foundation requires an investment in developing people from across the firm – not just fee earners or senior leaders.

Design thinking – A unifying framework for innovation

In recent years, a growing number of law schools and firms have looked to "design thinking" to equip lawyers and law students with the process, tools, and mindsets required to successfully innovate for their clients and within their firms.

Design thinking, an innovation framework used by some of the world's most consistently cutting edge companies, gives people a straightforward, practical approach to creative problem solving that can be applied to virtually any challenge (see Figure 1).

It starts by seeking to deeply understand what people (e.g. clients or internal customers) really value, need, and care about, and it applies a creative process and toolset to arrive at more innovative solutions for the challenges they face. Individuals trained in this approach learn how to use techniques such as effective questioning and empathy building, opportunity framing, brainstorming, and lateral thinking, as well as rapid prototyping and experimentation. With these core skills and mindsets instilled, every individual in the firm can be part of the innovation process. They become "listening posts" for opportunities to innovate both for clients and internal stakeholders.

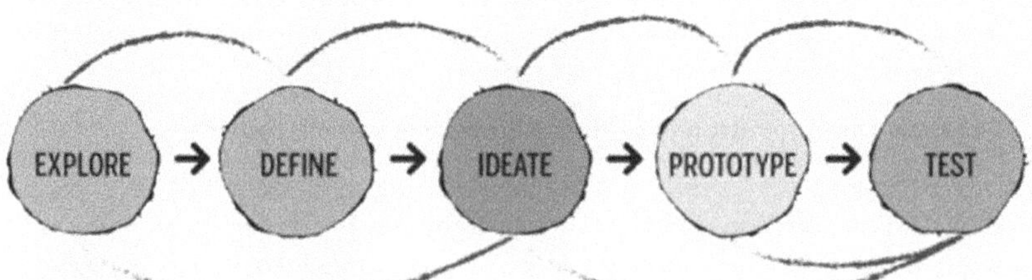

Figure 1: Design thinking – An innovation framework.

Legal sector innovation in action: Internal strategies

In the realm of internal innovation, there is a move towards more flexible time arrangements, as well as the provision of more structured training in areas beyond law, such as wider commercial skills for junior associates. Allen & Overy made the move to flexible working in 2010 and Linklaters allows lawyers to work from home one day per week. Simmons & Simmons has been recognized for its internal innovations, including the launch of its own MBA course in partnership with BPP business school, designed to prepare a new generation of lawyers with a range of legal and business skills.

They also become more confident in suggesting new ideas, secure in the knowledge that others understand the importance of deferring judgment and building on the ideas of others.

Meetings tend to become more focused on action and rapid iteration, rather than endless updates, and discussion and collaboration between disciplines become more fluid due to a shared toolset and approach to problem solving.

For many organizations, the most immediate benefits of equipping people with an innovative framework and toolkit like design thinking come from the way these techniques are applied in day-to-day work.

Small changes to the way individuals and teams organize and manage themselves can have a profound effect on the quality of work and the speed at which it is accomplished.

Making innovation skills development count

Leadership development and structured training can be powerful tools in building a culture of innovation, but there are several common pitfalls to avoid.

1. Don't just develop senior people.

What often happens is that a small cohort of senior leaders will go away for a day or so of innovation training and return to an organization that is not only oblivious to the concepts that they have learned, but in some cases geared to stamp them out. This makes applying and disseminating any of these new ideas very difficult, and despite best intentions, organizational inertia takes over and the status quo prevails.

Another problem with rolling these skills out to only a small group of senior leaders is that while their buy-in is required to establish a culture of innovation, it is not enough. The real work of innovation takes place on the front lines. These individuals also need to be engaged and on board before any real progress can be expected.

2. Don't just develop a small group of front-line innovators.

For many organizations, there is a temptation to invest heavily in developing the innovative capabilities of just a small group who will be tasked with driving innovation in the firm. These are frequently those people who are deemed to be "the innovative ones" – and could be partners or associates who have been flagged as future leaders or high potentials.

These groups are often tasked with projects, which when launched have strong top leadership support. But as projects continue, team members often face pressure from direct line managers to spend more time on their "real jobs" and are pulled away, resulting in stalled projects and disheartened would-be innovators.

Another danger of only developing small cohorts is that the way they will be working often won't make sense to their colleagues, and will therefore be rejected. Worse still, they may seek to involve senior people who haven't bought in to the value of seemingly counter-intuitive concepts like fast failure and rapid prototyping, and so end up getting criticized or "marked down" as a result.

Legal sector innovation in action: IT-driven innovation

In terms of IT-driven innovation, firms have used technology not only to reduce time and costs though automation, but also to enhance communication and facilitate collaboration, especially across offices. For example, Berwin Leighton Paisner has been able to assume responsibility for all the legal needs of some of its clients under multi-year, fixed-price agreements because it has built a multi-sourcing platform that supports BLP onsite teams. Technological innovations are also helping firms to provide longer term, more predictable fee estimates. Paul Hastings was recognized in 2015 for its development and deployment of a matter management system that improves efficiency and helps to give predictable fee estimates to clients.

Development initiatives are absolutely key to building a culture of innovation, but making them count takes real commitment. Not everyone in the firm needs to become an innovation expert, but virtually everyone needs to possess basic awareness of a shared framework, understand how innovation aligns with the business strategy, and be ready to support and encourage others.

Provide the right time, space, and funding

David Halliwell, director of knowledge, risk, and legal services for Pinsent Masons LLP, commented:

> *"Partners get out of bed to solve clients' problems, and those go beyond the specific transaction or need for advice in front of them. Where partners have time and space to think – and a client-led incentive to deliver – then innovation flies."*

Without making time to innovate, innovation is not likely to happen – at least not in any deliberate, reliable way. But what is the best way to do this in the time-starved environments of most law firms?

What kind of innovation do you want?

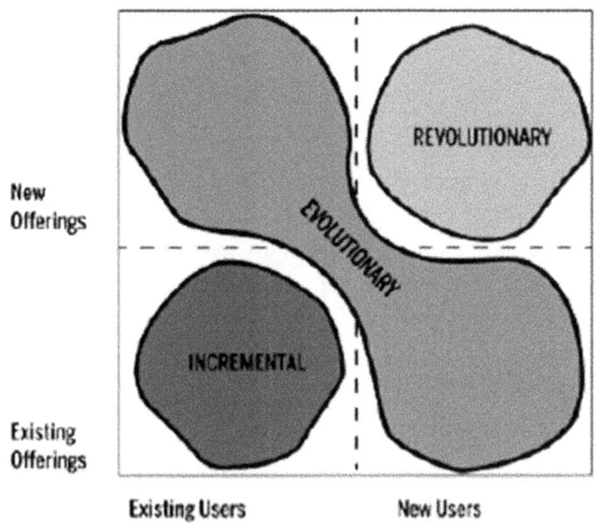

Figure 2: Categorizing innovation – Incremental, evolutionary, or revolutionary?

Knowing what kind of innovation will be most important for your firm can help inform the type of culture you need to achieve it, and the practical steps you need to take to build and sustain it. One simple way to look at different types of innovation is to divide them in to incremental, evolutionary, and revolutionary (see Figure 2).

Incremental innovations involve making changes to an existing service that is being delivered to an existing client. Examples of this might be a change in the way a service is priced or an added feature on an existing product. These innovations tend to be relatively low risk, and with little disruptive potential.

Evolutionary innovations involve diving into a new market or new product or service type. The firm might be entering adjacent markets, combining elements where the firm has existing expertise or relationships with others that are entirely new to it. Here, the risks as well as the potential for rewards are increased. Examples from the legal sector include Bird & Bird's Baseline and DLA Piper's Noble Street, where the firms offer non-legal advisory services in familiar markets.

Finally, there is the top right quadrant: revolutionary innovation. Here, the firm might be making a radical move into an entirely new service sector where the firm has no real experience. Innovations of this type are extremely high risk (often associated with greater than 90 percent failure rates) but have the highest potential for market disruption if they are successful. Depending on your strategy and risk appetite, your firm may tend towards one end of this spectrum more than another.

Strategies such as allowing a certain percentage of time per week to innovate have gained popularity, following examples from companies like Google and others of that ilk. However, our experience working with organisations that have implemented similar policies tells us that this approach often fails because:

- It is never fully implemented;
- Top leadership support isn't sustained;
- People lack the skills and tools to use the time in a useful way; or
- It is slowly eroded away by other projects that inevitably take higher priority.

Allowing time to innovate means allowing time to reflect – which in turn means removing high-priority tasks from the already overflowing plates of most fee earners and support staff.

Perhaps, one day, time spent on innovation will carry the same weight as meeting ambitious billing targets and deadlines for urgent client work. Until this happens, most law firms, and most corporates for that matter, are going to need to find other ways to make innovation happen.

Making innovation teams work

From our experience, even in organizations where innovation is widely encouraged at the individual level, there is no substitute for dedicated innovation teams when it comes to delivering on the full promise of innovation. Innovation teams might be formed of members drawn from across the firm on a rotation basis. The innovation project might, but does not need to be, the sole priority of members for a period of several weeks to multiple months. At the most basic level, successful innovation teams require:

- A clear brief. A well-framed opportunity and definition of what is in scope, what is not, and under what conditions the project should be extended or dropped.
- Sufficient funding. There is also no better way to demonstrate the firm's commitment to innovation than to visibly put real resources behind it. At the outset, make a budget available that is commensurate with the potential upside of the project, but encourage teams to develop the project through frequent low-cost experiments that lead to more developed pilots as learning is incorporated in each iteration.
- Diverse membership. The best teams are comprised of people with wide and varied skill sets from across practices, sectors, and offices – and not just lawyers. They might include business services people, administrators and managers, as well as clients and other contacts from outside the firm.
- A process to guide them. Innovation teams will struggle to make real progress using their traditional ways of working. Having a structured process to guide their thinking and working will improve outcomes and the ability for diverse teams to quickly and fluidly collaborate.
- A dedicated space for the project to live. Even if it is a space as humble as a single conference room or the corner of an office space, innovation projects tend to be more successful when teams have a fixed physical space to go to where they can be immersed in the project.
- A hands-off management approach. Innovation teams need to be managed and rewarded differently than teams focused on the core business of the firm. This requires a good deal of trust, empowerment, and permission to fail as long as the learning from

that failure is captured and applied to ensuring the next iteration is closer to success.

- Measurement that fits the task. A team working on a "revolutionary" innovation project (see Figure 2) shouldn't be measured in the same way as a team working on an incremental innovation, which has a far higher chance of success and is much closer to the firm's core business. Teams on high-risk projects could be rewarded, for example, not only for the success achieved, but also for the valuable lessons captured and shared with teams working on less risky projects.

Perhaps most importantly, successful innovation teams require the rest of the firm, especially senior leadership, to be on board with the team's purpose and the process they are using. This is the best way to ensure that the required time will be made available and respected in spite of competing priorities. Broad awareness and buy-in can also greatly reduce the risk of teams' interim work products and methods being evaluated by traditional measures and potentially getting quashed before they get off the ground.

Recognize common barriers to innovation

Innovation is not easy for anyone. It can create a fear of change and a resulting pulling up of the drawbridge. Actively or passively resisting change is, for some people, much more comfortable than managing the uncertainty that comes with something new.

Innovation can be especially hard for law firms with their business model still largely based on partner ownership, the billable hour, often strict hierarchies, and a long history of practicing law and running their business in a certain way. While there are no easy fixes, and change in most of these areas will be slow at best, it is vital to actively anticipate these roadblocks to innovation and use levers such as incentives, performance measurement systems, remuneration policy, and inspiring leadership to address them over time.

The billable hour

Innovation requires an "outside-in" mentality where the client is at the heart of the firm's strategy and service delivery model. The billable hour model is an example of "inside-out" thinking that is driven by what the firm is providing to the client as opposed to what they are creating for them or helping them achieve.

Andrew Giverin, sales director at Radiant Law, commented:

"From the client's point of view the legal sector is crying out for innovation. Everything pegged to billable hours encourages inefficiency. The billable hour is based on input not output or the value of what is generated. This makes it difficult to generate innovative ideas."

From this perspective, as well as in terms of measuring and rewarding innovation activities, the billable hour model presents significant challenges. A fee-earner's performance is primarily measured by billing levels, and innovation work is most often non-billable. In a delivery-focused culture, this creates a major hurdle for securing the time, resources, and support required to make innovation happen.

Hierarchies and power pockets

As well as the pressure of billable hours on lawyers, there is almost always an entrenched hierarchy in place, based on title, expertise, billing power, and years of post-qualification experience. Sometimes, as is the case within many groups of people, alliances and pockets of power can be partly hidden. For example, close colleagues who have moved en masse from other firms, friendships based on decades of working together, and cliques cemented by, say, godchildren or golf.

Innovation requires, if not a flat structure, a flat mentality that sets aside rank, role, and history. With partners at the top of decision-making tree, it may take real effort to create an environment, even if just a temporary one, where the ideas of a junior lawyer or business services manager have equal weight to those of a senior partner. It is, after all, not always the most senior people in the firm that will have the most revealing insights into emerging client needs or where internal process or cost efficiencies might be found.

Short-termism

Law firm leaders have to balance partner pressure for maximum short-term profit share against longer-term investment in innovation. Convincing partners exactly why they should care about and invest in innovation requires a compelling vision and strategy for success in both the short and long term. Client feedback, client requests, and a changing share of the client purse add weight here. In addition, regular competitive analysis, working to stay attuned to likely future market shifts, and monitoring trends in other sectors that might impact on longer-term service demand can help to reinforce the link between current innovation initiatives and future competitive advantage.

Bias for precision

Almost everything about the training and professional standing of lawyers encourages "getting things right", a fear of failure, and an aversion to making mistakes. Innovation requires most lawyers to change their mind-set or, metaphorically, to put on a different hat. Being able to flex between cautious, detail-oriented legal thinking and more risk-friendly and "bigger picture", innovation-related thinking requires self-awareness, sustained effort, and encouragement. Failure, when it inevitably happens, must not be seen as an "end", but rather a necessary step in an iterative process, and it must be recognized as a means of ultimately achieving success sooner.

Organizational structure

Here, structure is not only the central partnership model but also the systems and levers that make the business work – the groups, the hierarchy, reporting structure, information and decision-making channels, reward and promotion systems.

Innovation requires collaboration – and lots of it. Collaboration can be especially powerful when teams are drawn from diverse backgrounds, allowing for fresh perspectives and solutions to emerge.

Not all firms are structured in a way that enables great collaboration. In fact, some seem to be set up to almost deliberately encourage silos and internal competition, and collaborating across practice area or offices is often both difficult and frustrating.

Such barriers may exist due to implicit norms around sharing of information, cross-practice tension, cultural differences, a by-product of the reward system, or the "not invented here" mentality.

However, structure can also play to a firm's advantage. Cross-disciplinary collaboration is one of the benefits that can come from taking a sector-based approach – something claimed by many firms yet achieved by just a few.

Christian Bartsch, partner at Bird & Bird LLP, said:

"The culture at Bird & Bird is underpinned by a shared sense of natural curiosity. Our deep sector focus means that our lawyers are truly passionate about their sectors, sector-based budgeting encourages strong collaboration and our clients tend to be highly innovative themselves."

Lead by example and others will follow

Without leadership support, any effort to build a robust culture of innovation is very likely to fail. Influencing something as hard to pin down and measure as law firm culture requires committed and consistent leadership action in deeds as well as declarations. It takes a willingness to empower people across all levels of the firm, take risks, and accept and even embrace the ambiguity that comes with venturing into uncharted territory. While there are many attributes that a strong leader of innovation needs to possess, in our experience, there is none more powerful, or indispensable, than being a clear and visible role model. Creating and maintaining a culture of innovation requires unequivocal leadership modelling by law firm leadership and management teams on a day-to-day basis. This is a universe away from well-intentioned lip service and an annual innovation awards event. Innovation has to become a visible and integral part of business as usual from the top down.

Being a role model for innovation involves sharing regular and credible evidence of your commitment to promoting the best thinking of your people, to support them when they try in earnest and sometimes fail, and to publicly recognize them when their efforts bear fruit as learning or progress in whatever form.

Without trust that their innovation-related mindsets and behaviors will be welcomed rather than penalized, your talented workforce will likely:

- Continue to sit on potentially valuable ideas;
- Hold back their strong views and insights;
- Feel under-confident about discussing innovation with clients (leaving space for competitors to do so);
- Become frustrated and weaker ambassadors for your brand; and
- Be less inclined to collaborate internally and with clients towards creative and more innovative solutions.

This all adds up to a significant loss of competitive advantage. By showing, through body language, words, and deeds, and on a day-to-day basis, exactly how vital innovation is to the business, senior leaders can model the message a thousand times more effectively than any number of board papers, emails, or glossy brochures ever could. Successful innovation necessitates a "do as I do", not a "do as I say" leadership style.

Conclusion: Building a culture of innovation

If you and your firm are already building a culture of innovation, be sure to do it well. This is no subject for a shiny veneer or superficial commitment. Culture change is never fast or painless. However, creating an environment where innovation happens in a continuous, strategically aligned way can have a profound impact on a firm's long-term profitability and growth potential – especially in times of accelerating change. From our experience, this requires funding and actively supporting *both* firm-wide development initiatives *and* dedicated team-based innovation projects simultaneously. Omitting one dramatically limits the effectiveness of the other. When done together, they are mutually reinforcing. It also compels firms to take a close and honest look at those aspects of their existing culture, structure, and leadership style that might help or hinder a culture of innovation – and take meaningful steps to address them. Finally, law firms need to be open to learning from other sectors, and willing to adopt and adapt the right practices and frameworks in a way that is compatible with their uniquely delivery-focused and standards-driven environments.

David Halliwell, director of knowledge, risk and legal services for Pinsent Masons LLP, said:

> *"Law firms are the last businesses in the supply chain to be transformed. But being last is not such a bad thing. Law firms can learn quickly from other sectors and bring mainstream concepts newly to law to make business-changing progress quickly."*

The time is now. Don't procrastinate. Take small steps right now and fast – the advantages are enormous.

The ripple effect: Broader implications of an innovation culture

Innovation is relevant to every aspect of the business – not just to the development of new products and services or IT systems. As a culture of innovation grows within a firm, many of the practices and norms that we take for granted are likely to evolve along the way. Changes you might expect include, but are not limited to:

- The way you inspire, develop, empower, and reward your people;
- Greater likelihood of involving colleagues and clients in the very early stages of designing new products and services;

- The way people in the firm ask questions, actively listen and observe, and provide feedback;
- Communicating value, scope, and pricing options clearly and in a way that meets agreed rather than assumed client needs;
- Your style of leadership and management approach;
- Greater attention paid to the innovations of competitors, including new entrants who have based their entire model on technology, client service, and innovation;
- The way you collaborate internally and externally, including investing time in building diverse networks and listening to different perspectives;
- The way you encourage ideas, manage expectations about how they will be used, develop prototypes, and respond to "failure";
- Greater appetite to learn from other sectors about trends and different ways of doing things;
- Overcoming the tendency to hold on to work that can, over time, be more profitably and efficiently done elsewhere or in a different way;
- Having greater leadership support or authority to move at speed to capitalize on small-window opportunities to meet client needs ahead of competitors; and
- Ensuring that everyone in the firm understands their part in the bigger picture – the link between their work and the specific client benefit.

What changes might you expect to see in your firm?

With thanks to colleagues, Garth Olcese and Duncan Brannan.

Chapter 5:

Beliefs, attitude, and values that encourage "innovation thinking"

By Duncan Hart, barrister

To be innovative by my definition requires that a number of key behaviors be developed and deployed by the firm's personnel, particularly its leadership team. These include the following.

Curiosity, empathy, and an openness of mind:

- An acute sensitivity to the needs, problems, and emerging needs of the clients you seek to serve;
- A knowledge and curiosity about the wider economic and other forces impacting the economy as a whole;
- A knowledge and curiosity about how innovation and change are managed in other organizations, particularly those other service providers that may also be providing services to your clients;
- A readiness to review all facets of your firm's strategy and business model, and to take nothing for granted; and
- A clear idea of what your competitors and potential competitors are doing.

Team work and leadership:

- A willingness to allow employees to actively participate in shaping the environment in which they work, which must be matched by management's willingness to listen, act, and support their initiatives;
- A willingness to adopt new ways of performing essential tasks and a readiness to be self-critical of "how things are (usually) done around here";
- A good understanding about how to inspire, motivate, and follow through the introduction of what might be quite disruptive changes

in the firm's structures, processes, and even its business model as a whole; and

- Capacity to work across different practice groups, jurisdictions, and specialties.

Risk tolerance:

- A willingness to test and review innovative changes, and the courage to close down those which are not working as hoped and to invest and develop further those that are; and
- Capacity to suffer reversals, delays, and failures in an endeavor to drive innovation processes and outcomes.

I describe these behaviors, attitudes, and values as characteristics of "innovation thinking", a necessary pre-condition to what can be described as "innovation analysis", and eventually "innovation action". The latter simply represents the disciplines of actually implementing effectively the outcomes of your innovation thinking and analysis. Undue emphasis is too often placed upon the "Eureka" event, that moment of incandescent intensity that suddenly lights the way forward. Such a perspective overlooks the sheer hard work in putting in place the processes and respecting the thinking, analysis, processes, and behaviors that contributed or led to that moment. These include the openness of mind, the appreciation of the need to be alert to the market and the wider forces shaping the environment, the impact of technology, the broader state of the economy, the demographics and skills of your work force, and the expertise that may be directly applicable to your firm but already applied in different sectors. Similarly, it ignores the sheer hard work, leadership, and processes required to sort the "light bulbs" from the "damp squibs" and the difficulty in fanning embers of inspiration into infrequent fiery success. This is the even harder work of "innovation action".

Success in innovation is perhaps best summarized as "fortune favoring the prepared mind".[1] I would broaden that to include not only the "mind" but also the organization as a whole, or at least its key leadership elements. A "prepared" mind and organization must also develop key behaviors around its innovation initiatives, such as:

- An appreciation of the need to innovate and keep innovating;
- The courage to experiment and suffer even public reversals when initiatives fail;

- A willingness to invest obviously, both materially and emotionally in innovative processes within the firm; and
- A willingness to invest in innovative activities in conjunction with clients, third parties, and even potential competitors.

These qualities in combination with the beliefs, attitudes, and values mentioned above facilitate the breeding ground of good ideas. As Thomas J. Watson, the founder of IBM, observed, "the best way to have a good idea is to have lots of them".

The thinking process then requires a certain commitment to individual, organizational, and externally orientated practices and processes. It is from those attitudes and behaviors that one should strive to develop the initial crop of ideas that are to be nurtured to maturity or discarded in preference to more promising alternatives. In short, the ground must be prepared before there is any real hope of embarking on the difficult task of transforming ideas into useful innovations, be they modest or transformative in their impact.

I emphasize the need for preparatory action at those three levels because it is almost inevitable that, without it, no matter how promising any initiative might be, it will often fail. What is worse, the memory of failure, particularly public failure, can become woven into the fabric of a firm's collective memory. In other words, even one failure can create a long lasting knee-jerk response. I have heard so often, "we tried that once and it didn't work". This is often then applied to almost every initiative that is suggested and which requires some change to "the way things are done around here". Professionals are usually paid to be "right", and while they are often prepared to risk quite a lot on their client's behalf, they are notoriously conservative when it comes to their own businesses![2]

Having said that, firms are frequently convulsed by dramatic changes driven by individual or organizational issues or, more commonly, by client and competitive pressures. Many of these changes are for the better and can be classed as "innovative", but many are not and are achieved at great cost to the organization. How should organizations not only attempt to manage such rapid changes, but even use such events to drive a more constructive and less damaging process?

So how is the ground best prepared for innovation? There are several scenarios that present a leader or any group of partners seeking to develop their innovation agenda with the opportunity to create opportunities through a more disciplined approach to innovation. Some are clearly more desirable than others, however.

Common incentives to encourage innovation thinking

The firm or team crisis

The most common motivator for innovation, which I have already raised, is a crisis. There is much truth in Machiavelli's observation that one should "never waste a good crisis". This is the time when leaders and good ideas frequently emerge, driven by the urgency of the situation, and often accompanied by a willingness of the wider group to implement or "try anything". Attractive as this may appear initially, the dangers of suddenly implementing the first "good idea" in the heat of the moment are obvious.

In this situation, it is far preferable of course to have a series of innovations already under active consideration which are often simply awaiting such a crisis in order to be introduced or, even better, are or have been trialed in anticipation of just such an event. Every crisis will present different opportunities for, and demands of, any organization and timing is critical in such circumstances. This may appear to be wishful thinking, but every group should always be prepared to face such "what if" question squarely. Of itself, this attitude of "taking nothing for granted" often drives a constructive approach to embracing innovation thinking in a group on a systematic basis. Certainly, the need for such induced drama waxes and wanes with the fortunes of the group concerned but can be a very useful prod to encourage the development of the type of approach and behaviors I am advocating.

More frequent than a firm-wide crisis, such as that resulting from say a 2008 "general financial crisis" type event, is that created by the loss of key team members in a specific area, legislative change, or the loss of a major client. These more localized or limited crises can provide an ideal test bed for innovation programs. Ideally, if the team has been exposed to the need for innovation thinking before such a crisis emerges, then the better prepared they will be to meet its particular challenges.

A client crisis

Crises are often experienced at a client level. A sudden demand for a dramatically lower price of service offering, a tender which appears to ask for the impossible, a client threatening to depart if major changes are not instituted. Clients also routinely review their legal costs and consider the merits of bringing their work "in house", often taking the best of the firm's personnel that service them with them.

In short, when it comes to clients, there are no shortages of possible scenarios which can substantially disrupt any firm and impact profitability and morale adversely. The options available to clients as to how and where they seek legal advice continue to grow. This not only includes "outsourcing" work to cheaper jurisdictions, but also the ability of clients to set up their own "law firm", as has been seen in the ABS structures now permitted in some jurisdictions. At the consumer level, there is a raft of websites – of which LegalZoom[3] is a prominent example – offering an increasing range of pre-packaged solutions for those seeking cheaper options. Clients are also receptive to the "unbundling" of services, once offered "end to end" by a law firm, but now distributed amongst many suppliers reducing the law firm's role and their profits.

Change of leadership

This is thankfully becoming a more accepted and orderly practice in most professional service firms. Commonly, it occurs by election, rotation, or the introduction of an outside "CEO" or management professional. It can also be driven in a merger environment, a change in the structure of the firm by, say, incorporation, or by the introduction of a managing team, as opposed to an individual being responsible for the firm's leadership.

This then presents distinct opportunities to introduce a program of innovation thinking. Rather than approach the issue in a relatively timid fashion, the new leader or leadership team should embark on a more ambitious program than mere tinkering at the fringes. Undoubtedly, there will be numerous changes that such a leadership change might provoke, but that should not be seen as the end point.

It should herald a more ambitious program, which continually asks and promotes an examination of the need for innovation of all types and looks for opportunities to demonstrate it.

Strong and enlightened leadership which brings with it the ability and determination to introduce the processes, incentives, and other policies required to progress any "innovation agenda" is the single most important contributor to the success of any such agenda, particularly at this early stage.

A "lost" initiative

Most firms have had one or more innovative initiatives lurking in the footnotes of their strategic plans or tucked away in the "wish lists" of influential partners. Many, curiously enough, are never implemented because they seldom see the light of day, or if they do there is lack of support, timidity, or timing issues. In many cases, it is the result of fear of failure, i.e. "we will only do (or even suggest) that if things really get bad", and that time never seems to arrive, or if it does it is far too late to take such an initiative forward.

On occasions, however, pressure within specific groups, an ambitious team leader or senior associate will surface the initiative or "run it up the flag" on behalf of, or in conjunction with, a partner. These occasions can also be an opportune time to "springboard" a more comprehensive program using this particular initiative as one of a series of "experiments" to introduce the wider concept of innovation to other teams within the firm.

Is there a more "strategic" approach?

A crisis may provide the urgency and the support for an innovation initiative, or at least a "honeymoon" period for such a wider approach. An established leader or leadership team should not assume, however, that without a crisis attitude any attempt will be frustrated. While it is often thought that the pressure for such change will come from below, this is seldom seen in my experience, and I strongly encourage the view that such changes must be led, driven, and supported at the highest level in the organization. Far better for the chances of sustainable change if the organization, or substantial parts of it, is receptive to such a program, but I am assuming that in the majority of cases this will not be the case. Those that might in the past have supported, or even led, such initiatives have often departed in frustration or been attracted to more aggressively innovative firms.

Resistance in various forms must always be factored into any innovation initiative. Realistically, I do not suggest that all teams will suddenly "come on board" as the benefits of an innovation program are promoted by the leadership team. A firm is often said to have its own in-built "immune" system which must be continually confronted.

Innovation as I've described it requires change, risk, and even a willingness to cannibalize the firm's existing business model for the uncertain benefits of untried alternatives. Resistance is thus almost guaranteed!

A predictable range of such immune responses must be catered for:

- Skepticism about any management-led initiative;
- A desire to see much greater detail than is realistically possible given the experimental nature of the initiative being promoted;
- Passive resistance – i.e. "they" can do what they like but "we" won't be changing anything about the way we work in our particular area;

- Arguments that there are more pressing priorities, and that any initiative should be reviewed later or be subject to the all too familiar strategy of "death by committee";
- Begrudging approval, but with such tight constraints as to make any initiative more than likely stillborn;
- Generational resistance from older or soon to be departing partners unwilling to invest because of the likely impact on short-term profitability;
- Unhappiness about the specific initiative being put forward as the first experiment or the people likely to be involved in it – i.e. preference for their particular favorite; or
- A desire to introduce too much oversight or control which will cripple the implementation process.

Dealing with the firm's immune system

To deal with the firm's immune system and to tackle the challenges that an innovation agenda presents requires a more measured approach which:

- Alerts the firm to the need for an innovation agenda (why would we do this and what are we going to be expected to contribute?);
- Inspires a group or at least a few key individuals to act as a test bed for the program's immediate aims;
- Calms initial fears that many will feel about the immediate impact such a program may have on their particular group;
- Discourages passive resistance by focusing initially on the "true believers";
- Carefully spells out how cooperation, input, expense, and evaluation of any innovative initiative will proceed;
- Outlines a test or pilot program using a specific example which demonstrates how the program will work (at least in its first phase);
- Points to examples in the market which may demonstrate a model you wish to follow or adapt, or one which obviously represents a threat to the firm; and
- Points out how the development of initiatives will be taken forward, emphasizing how that is a different process from that which may have led to failures in the past.

This approach should be developed to avoid the pitfalls of a crisis-driven response, preparing the firm to adopt a more disciplined and informed methodology in developing and implementing its innovation agenda.

References

1. Attributed to Louis Pasteur, inventor of pasteurization.
2. See generally, Argyris, C., "Teaching Smart People How to Learn", *Harvard Business Review*, May–June 1991, available at: https://hbr.org/1991/05/teaching-smart-people-how-to-learn
3. www.legalzoom.com

Chapter 6:

Innovative pricing – The gap between clients' expectations and law firms' delivery

By Chris Howe, director at Raedbora Consulting

Pricing in the legal industry

As we all know, pricing in the legal industry has developed over recent decades to become dominated by the use of the hourly rate. This was not always the case, but the modern "default" has been to price using records of hours spent by lawyers on the matter in question. While lawyers were in demand and firms simply had to "throw open the doors" and work would flood in, this was just fine for the lawyers. No great thought was required to set pricing – one simply referred to the firm's published rate card and calculated the fee.

Clients effectively had no choice if they were to get the work done. Lawyers undoubtedly missed opportunities to charge premiums when clients got the benefit of years of experience in a few minutes' advice which saved them large sums, but in general lawyers were the main beneficiaries with high profit levels coupled with very limited commercial risk as clients were effectively paying "cost plus".

This landscape has of course completely changed since the downturn created significant challenges for some firms, but also some opportunities. While the legal press has focused on "the end of the hourly rate" and lower prices, there has been relatively little comment on the way clients are using the change in the balance of power to shift the balance of risk too. This is likely to be a permanent change in the legal landscape and it requires innovative approaches to both the client relationship and pricing – innovative, that is for legal! In this chapter, we will look at clients' frustrations and how they are driving changes that some parts of the industry are not ready for.

The client perspective

The shift in the balance of supply and demand has allowed buyers greater influence not only over the level of price but also the nature of the agreement between the client and the lawyer. As we noted above, lawyers have been pricing with virtually no commercial risk for years, expecting the client to take the impact of all unexpected events. These can range from bad estimating through to ineffective or inefficient work. Also, external events can throw a project off track through no fault of either the client or lawyer. The only risk sitting with the lawyer was the risk arising from poor advice.

There are plenty of examples of clients' frustration with the overall commercial service provided by lawyers. I see this at many of the firms I deal with. In one notable example, feedback I saw went as follows: "You quoted £100,000 for the job. There was no further discussion about fees until the bill arrived. When that showed a bill of £400,000 you made me look an idiot as I had to go back to the Board for authorization for the extra money after the event."

This illustrates a number of points:

- Lawyers need to be good project managers as well as legal experts – and that includes tracking progress and reporting changes early;
- Lawyers must understand how their client works and adapt to it. In many industries "no surprises" is the watchword;
- There is an assumption that the client will take all overruns. If we are seeking to align our interests with clients and build long term relationships, is this sustainable?
- Unexpected changes either by the client or by third parties are no excuse for slack management of a project or fees.

I understand that in this case the legal team had done a fantastic job in trying circumstances – but was the client satisfied?

How clients choose a law firm

In order to understand more the behaviors we should be adopting, it is instructive to consider how clients would like to choose their legal adviser vis-à-vis how they actually choose. To do this I have drawn on real experience of panel reviews from the client side of the table, and interview with GCs.

Whether a client uses a panel or has no panel and instructs directly to the market, the challenge remains to select the best overall offer for a particular matter. This assessment will be a mix of quality, delivery, and cost considerations with a view to maximizing the total value of the entire project.

Immediately it is clear that, if all the facts are available, lowest cost is certainly not a primary concern. If a relatively small amount of extra spend on lawyers will increase the overall value of the project by a much larger amount, or mitigate some significant risks, this is a desirable outcome. This logic quickly leads to the concept of "value pricing", whereby the law firm justifies their additional fee by reference to the "value added" to the overall project rather than the hours worked. Law firms would do well to remember, however, that wherever two law firms provide the same value add, the client will still choose the cheapest offer, all other things being equal.

In practice though, clients are often not able to identify or establish just how one firm will add value compared to another. When asked how he chose between firms, one panel manager told me: "We can't really. We go off reputation and past experience, and of course price." No surprise then that clients are often reluctant to change provider. At least that way any minimum requirements on quality or delivery are likely to be met.

From the law firm's perspective, it is often difficult to break into new work areas and clients. "Differentiation" is a key word heard in many business development departments, but more rarely does a client see a truly differentiated, and relevant, offer presented to them.

Conversely, getting clients to specify properly the requirement is quite a challenge, meaning that any good scoping work that does go on could be built on flawed foundations. Many firms just take this risk and quote anyway but a situation where the client doesn't know what they are asking for, and the law firm doesn't know what they are taking on, is hardly desirable.

What do clients really want?

Client survey work shows that pricing *per se* is not in the top five concerns for clients – contrary to what we may all have thought. Value for money, however, is in that top five. Clients of course increasingly ask lawyers about innovative pricing – and indeed it has become almost *de rigeur* to include such a question in panel reviews. Notwithstanding, the response from law firms is often inadequate and rarely does an "innovative" proposal truly provide a means for a client to properly evaluate it against alternatives.

Ideally a client would be able to compare pricing from different firms with a clear understanding that either these prices were provided against a consistent understanding of the scope, or that where there are differences these can be easily identified and their impact understood.

Clients are growing increasingly intolerant of facing a large quote or estimate and having to rely on reputation or prior experience as the only other real criteria. They are also much less forgiving when conversations after the event take place seeking to bill overruns. Any unexpected costs are bad news in the corporate world.

An increasing number of clients are relying on fixed or capped fees in an attempt to try to manage these risks, but only with limited success as lawyers have sometimes responded with very tight and rigorous lists of risks and assumptions. One could be forgiven for thinking some of these risks were more likely to happen than not happen, and that the assumptions are based on some Alice-in-Wonderland world where nothing goes wrong!

Other firms think that agreeing to fixed fees and then sticking to it means that the pricing problem is somehow resolved. As I pointed out to one partner recently, all this means is that the risk of overrun has just moved into the law firm – and is unknown without careful scoping. He went rather pale at that last observation!

Another partner told me that they couldn't scope work because they didn't know what was going to be involved in the work – yet seemed happy to agree fixed fees running into seven digits.

None of this really helps us get to a place where:

- Clients are clear on the work they require;
- Law firms scope and set out what they plan to do;
- Clients can see what they are paying for, rather than who is doing it;
- Risks are clearly understood; and
- Most importantly there is a clear and transparent understanding of the baseline from which we are all starting.

Variations are therefore much clearer, and their causes can be more clearly seen and attributed. Some innovation in scoping and pricing is therefore clearly needed.

What is innovation?

We therefore get to the nub of what innovative pricing really means. There is no point in innovation for innovation's sake. It may get headlines in the legal press – read by other lawyers – but does not necessarily align you with your client's interest.

In another salient example, I remember the bidding team responding to a question about innovative pricing with a striking and bold offer which, while containing some considerable commercial risk, offered big opportunities for both the client and the law firm. The response the team got was "in the nicest possible way, you've called our bluff on 'innovative' pricing". The offer was too innovative for the client to digest, but it did demonstrate the team's ability to think outside the box, and was viewed favorably.

A great definition of innovation that is widely accepted is:

> *Innovation is the development of new values through solutions that meet new requirements, inarticulate needs, or old customer and market needs in value adding new ways. Innovation differs from invention in that innovation refers to the use of a better and, as a result, novel idea or method, whereas invention refers more directly to the creation of the idea or method itself. Innovation differs from improvement in that innovation refers to the notion of doing something different rather than doing the same thing better.*[1]

So, in developing innovative pricing methods we should look first to solutions that meet our client needs more effectively. We do not have to create these methods from scratch but simply use approaches we find elsewhere – perhaps in other industries. Proper understanding of your client is critical. Conversely, simply reducing prices is not innovative.

What does constitute innovative pricing and how do we achieve it?

Clearly, each truly innovative arrangement will be specific to the parties involved and the circumstances of the deal. However, the common elements of successful deals can be summarized easily. For me the key elements of an innovative pricing solution in legal are:

- Proper understanding of the client's requirement and the law firm's requirement translated into the commercial agreement between the parties;
- Value for money in all outcomes, taking into account appropriate reward for risks taken;
- Clear and simple so easily understood; and
- Takes account of the competition, their capabilities, and their competing prices.

Finally, any pricing decision should then test whether the work can be done profitably, and more particularly how the work can be organized to maximize profit. Pricing using hourly rates achieves none of the above.

You no doubt get a sense that my view is that what we now regard as "innovative" should, and will quickly, become the norm. We will know when we get there when we stop referring to "innovative pricing" and "alternative fee arrangements". These terms imply that such pricing approaches are unusual – only in legal. A brief consideration of how you buy all your other goods and services either as an individual or a business will quickly show you that actually it is legal hourly rates that is the "alternative" or unusual approach.

Solutions

Fortunately, help is at hand. There are a number of technical solutions to assist firms with planning and margin management. Solutions can be obtained which, given the right data entry, will allow a detailed understanding of where margin has been lost – provided the starting budget is clearly understood. There are also solutions which enable accurate costing – providing the scale of the matter has been worked out.

Relatively few, however, deal with the key element – which is scoping out the work to be done in the first place. Such a solution needs to:

- Ensure all the key elements required to deliver the work have been included;
- Ensure those that are not required are excluded(!);
- Estimate the effort involved in each component of the solution; and
- Get buy-in and agreement with the client as to what is "in" or "out" of the scope of work.

With these elements confirmed, pricing, managing, and monitoring become the easier parts of the equation.

Scoping work

Solutions are now becoming available that deal with exactly this issue. New software tools allow lawyers to scope and price directly and quickly from work templates, establishing in the scoping work an understanding of what is to be done from the outset.

A number of clients are now seeing these approaches as a way both to manage their internal processes in order to ensure a clear work specification, but also as a means of competitively tendering work within their existing panel.

The key point to note is the shift from "who" will do the work to "what" will be delivered to the client, and the value of that output.

What is in it for the client?

Clients can now have the opportunity to evaluate bids on a transparent basis focused on delivery rather than reputation. A client can compare different bids on a consistent basis. Finally, when left to "promote" the business case for the work internally, the in-house lawyer is equipped with a good degree of substance with which to make the case and demonstrate value. These elements go a long way to enabling the client to make a balanced decision on quality, delivery, *and* cost.

What is in it for the law firm?

The law firm can quickly define upfront the true scope of the matter, potentially in tandem with the client. Software tools now allow an early price to be generated "on the move" without need to refer to support analysts and spreadsheets. Robust scopes and prices can be generated against consistent approaches to work, managing quality control and developing consistency. Where work appears unprofitable, this is visible during the immediate scoping stage – allowing decisions when they matter, rather than when it is too late. The ability to demonstrate consistent procedure when scoping work will in itself benefit firms by adding "weight" to their proposals.

For early adopters, these solutions provide an opportunity for the firm to *demonstrate* rather than *assert* it is truly innovative – i.e. using new solutions to meet an existing need in a different way – and responding positively to clients' demand for transparency.

Where next for innovative client relationships?

Whatever the particular mechanism used, clients will increasingly insist on this transparency, and if law firms do not provide it, clients will find different mechanisms to enforce it.

The law firms who are first to adopt the new paradigm and demonstrate it to clients with enthusiasm will have a significant competitive edge. In due course, though, all firms will need to adopt this more transparent and objective approach.

The only question really is: are you ready to be one of the first, or will you be in the following pack, or worst of all left behind altogether?

Reference

1. Innovation Management and Process of Innovation Management – Patil and Athavale from *Redefining Management Practices and Marketing in Modern Age*

Chapter 7: Developing knowledge capability to support innovation

By Mark Gould, founder of Mark Gould Consulting

Innovation is rooted in knowledge, combined with creativity and imagination. This combination is also critical to good legal advice: helping clients achieve their goals within the constraints imposed by the law.

Unlike legal advice, however, transformative innovations may not have easily identifiable client demand. Deep change also depends on the firm itself being geared towards innovation as a core activity, rather than relying on ideas being generated randomly.

Innovative people will always have good ideas. The real challenge for law firms is to cultivate innovation better. That has two parts:

- Transforming people and teams that cannot or will not innovate so that they come up with new ideas; and
- Taking ideas from all sources and developing them into marketable products or services.

Creating a culture within which innovation is a natural expectation for all in the firm is a hard task. To achieve that goal, firms need to think differently about knowledge.

Innovation basics

Innovation doesn't take place in a vacuum. In order to be of any use, good ideas have to be recognized and valued by someone other than the person with the idea. In most cases this will be clients, but the firm itself might be the intended beneficiary. Truly useful changes are marked by the value they bring. "Innovation" is best thought of as "an improvement that meets a real need". That need might be external (improving client service, for example) or internal (where a change in working practices results in improvements to profit).

For these purposes, the possible improvements that firms might make can be separated into four types:

1. Innovation in the law itself (providing a novel legal solution to client's legal or business problem);
2. New products or services developed for clients at the practice group level;
3. Improvements that completely change the way the firm works with clients (client service delivery); and
4. Improvements in the way the firm runs that are invisible to clients (internal operations).

Of these types of innovation, the first depends on an explicit client need and simply requires an imaginative lawyer to act on the opportunity presented by the client. Such innovations could occur in any firm. The others require the firm to be supportive of experimentation (not all ideas succeed) and change (successful initiatives require old ways of working to be put aside).

Traditional law firms often find it hard to tolerate experimentation and change, especially when they have an annual cycle of budgeting and investment. New forms of legal business, which can often take a longer view, may have a greater capacity for innovation as a result. Resistance to experimentation also explains why a small number of business-focused changes (legal project management, different pricing models, use of paralegals and other resourcing models) occur in a large number of firms. These improvements are based on business practices outside the law, and have been proven in use. As firms see them introduced elsewhere, they can see the benefits in action and copy their peers.

Whatever innovation process a firm has, there will be some key stages that depend heavily on knowledge and knowledge- related skills. The following are particularly worthy of note:

- Generation of ideas;
- Assessment of likely impact of the new idea (whatever form it might take); and
- Evaluation of possible market reaction.

Each of these stages demands different types of knowledge or insight, mobilized in different ways. That knowledge or insight may contribute to the idea itself, the need for the improvement, or both. Firms wanting a more innovative culture therefore need to concentrate on fostering the right knowledge activities and habits.

Table 1 shows more precisely the kinds of questions firms may need to answer by drawing on knowledge.

	Ideas	Impact	Reaction
Legal solutions	What knowledge do we have to solve novel client problems?	What do we know to help judge the likely success of solutions we propose?	Do we have enough experience and distinctive knowledge to found a new practice area?
Products/ services	Which know-how is most suitable for packaging, and what kind of delivery mechanisms are possible?	Do clients want this – is there a need and does it fit with their existing systems?	What is the future for this product or service? How can we sustain it or develop it when it is copied?
Client service	How could we meet our clients' needs better? What do we know about what might be within our (legal and other) capabilities?	What are our clients' needs (not just those expressed directly, but also those implicit in their behavior and market context)?	What are the implications for the firm if we are successful in changing the way we deliver client service? How might the market react and what else might need to change?
Internal operations	Where do we perform well, and where poorly? What could be different?	What are our needs (not just those expressed directly, but also those implicit in our behavior and market context)?	What are the implica-tions for the firm if we are successful in changing the way it works? How might the market react, and what else might need to change?

Table 1: Questions that draw on knowledge to drive innovation.

Knowledge management and innovation

Left to their own devices, good lawyers will always come up with good new ways of working with their clients. Better, more consistent results come when the firm has established tools, techniques, and processes to make it easier for good lawyers to follow their instincts and for others to reach the standard of the good ones. No modern law firm should rely solely on the instincts of their people – they need to intervene to improve performance. That is one of the core functions of knowledge management (KM) in law firms.

Law firms have traditionally approached KM by concentrating on gathering and improving access to legal know-how and lawyers' expertise and experience. This kind of legal KM ensures that lawyers can do work of the same type more effectively on successive occasions. That leads to the creation of resources such as banks of standard documents, training programs, know-how repositories, search engines, and expertise locators. Those things will always remain important, and may themselves be the subject of innovation (by using established knowledge more intelligently in the form of automated documents, client self-service products, and so on).

KM activities of this type are inherently backward-looking. They capture historic activities and present them to lawyers as a guide for future use. If that future use is identical to the past, the resource in question will obviously be valuable. If the future use is dissimilar, but the lawyer is intelligent, the resource may be helpful as a guide. Traditional KM resources can therefore help support the generation of ideas in response to client need. This is because those ideas depend heavily on what lawyers know about the law itself. They can also help lawyers assess how successful the idea might be in achieving the client's goals, as that might be underpinned by an understanding of previous court decisions or successful negotiating positions. Those facts might be noted in a good KM system, or other experts within the firm (identified using an expertise locator, for example) might be able to provide the requisite guidance.

Once clients have been advised on novel legal issues, that information should find its way into the firm's knowledge system. If other clients bring similar queries, the knowledge system should be updated with more detailed information about the topic – perhaps even including standard documents or anonymized examples of client advice. As it becomes clearer that there is an appreciable market for advice of this type, a new practice group might be established. The development and success of this group would depend on a number of things, including the existence of critical knowledge resources. The knowledge system therefore contributes to an assessment of and reaction to market needs.

This sequence of events provides an example of the first type of legal innovation. It also matches Richard Susskind's now well-known description of the evolution of legal services. Novel advice is initially bespoke to a particular client, but then becomes standardized with repetition, and then systematized into a new practice area. All these steps take place within the firm. Clients will benefit, but there may be no fundamental change in the way they are serviced by the firm. The next stage in Susskind's description (the packaging of legal advice) is also supported by traditional KM, but its impact is more obvious to clients. In being packaged, firms' legal insight is turned into products or services that clients can use without instructing a lawyer.

Using existing knowledge from within the firm to create new legal services or products might represent an improvement to clients, but legal knowledge alone is insufficient for innovation of this type. In order to transcend existing distillations of legal knowledge, such as bulletins, briefings, or training sessions, a new product or service needs to be packaged in a novel fashion. This might mean using an existing delivery mechanism in a new way or using a completely new method. Selecting the right approach will often depend on insight that lawyers do not have. Instead, firms will need to use non-legal knowledge that is not usually found in their KM systems.

Examples of this kind of innovation abound in the law – long-standing examples include the Out-Law service from Masons (now Pinsent Masons) and Linklaters' online term sheet generator. Each of these embedded existing legal knowledge practices within novel forms of delivery so that clients (and others) could use the firm's know-how without a lawyer acting as intermediary.

Traditional KM activities support the development of creative legal solutions for individual clients and their evolution into standalone practice areas. However, firms need additional input to create more wide-ranging innovations. This is true for packaged products and services – while lawyers are well placed to decide that certain content is ripe for packaging, it is increasingly unlikely that they will be the best people to decide the form that package (the delivery mechanism) should take.

A focus on legal material also means that traditional KM is incapable of helping firms judge the likelihood of success of a novel product or service by reference to whether or not it meets client needs. If an innovation of this type is successful with clients, other firms in the market will react by copying it or by innovating in different directions. Legal KM can't help firms plan how to respond to those market reactions.

In general, then, the approach to knowledge management adopted by most law firms can only assist with the most basic innovations. Firms that want to do something genuinely new above and beyond this level have to approach knowledge differently. In particular, they need to learn how to access the less visible knowledge within the firm and combine it with other insights to create something that hasn't existed before.

A different approach: Improving knowledge capability

Innovations in client service delivery and internal operations fundamentally change the way a firm works. Such changes need to be rooted in a deep understanding of the firm and its market, its clients and their markets, and broader technical environmental issues. This demands an approach to knowledge that goes beyond KM as firms have traditionally understood it. Such an approach has been defined by David Griffiths (a specialist in this area) as knowledge capability:

> *"... the ability to deploy knowledge to constantly design, develop, deliver, and maintain products and/or services that its current and future stakeholders will find valuable – put another way, an organization's Knowledge Capability is an indicator of its adaptive capability (its ability to anticipate (sense) and react to change)."*

As described already, traditional KM tends to concentrate on gathering and redeploying what is already known. This is an answer-focused approach. A standard document or practice note is defined in part by the purposes to which it will be put. It is presented as an answer to predictable questions. In addition, good lawyers might use KM material as indirect aids in unpredicted but comparable situations.

Other KM resources have a similar function. For example, lawyer profiles in an expertise database are written with existing needs in mind – they provide possible answers to questions that are already understood, such as "who is our expert in this area of law?" They work less well when the questions are more unexpected, such as "how can we work better with clients in this novel sector?"

It is essential that firms have these traditional answer-focused resources at the foundation of their knowledge strategy. Without them, there would be too many inefficiencies for the firm to survive, let alone be in a position to assist clients with novel legal problems. However, the state of the legal market now means that mere survival is not enough. In the face of intensified competition, client pressure on fees and performance, and regulatory change, no firm can thrive merely by doing what it currently does more efficiently.

Unlike traditional KM activities, frameworks for developing knowledge capability tend to prioritize questions rather than answers. This is a cultural change as much as an organizational strategy. In order for a firm to make the most of a question-focused approach, a number of characteristics are needed. The most important of these are connectivity, openness, and trust.

We have already seen how connections within a firm can assist in producing useful ideas. When considering packaging legal knowledge into new products and services, lawyers depend on the insight of others in the firm. These could include technologists, marketers, learning professionals, or anyone who might have a fresh perspective on what would help clients. At present, these connections have to be made deliberately: the lawyer needs to be aware of someone who could help and ask them directly. A better approach would be to improve the general level of awareness of work that is being done across the firm so that people can volunteer their help when they see that it might be needed. Firms that ensure that all their people can see what is being done for clients (within the bounds of confidentiality), and encourage the general sharing of insights of all types, are more likely to see a higher rate of successful innovations. In all areas of life and work, novel ideas often occur when someone sees something in an unrelated area that resonates in their own.

Better connectivity across the firm is an essential starting point for improving knowledge capability. However, the improved connections need to have some substance in them. Like electrical cables or water pipes, they need to be filled with something that can flow around the firm. Within a firm, good connections between people improve the flow of information.

That information could be anything that is even tangentially relevant to the firm's work. It would certainly include information about clients and their sectors, but for maximum value firms also need to be transparent about more sensitive things like financial data at a fairly detailed level, or unedited feedback provided by clients.

When people have greater visibility of the firm's performance and reflections about the work done across the firm, sometimes known as "working out loud", they can make better informed decisions about their own work. They can also offer support to others when previously they might not have known that their assistance would have been useful. Without openness and transparency, those opportunities for innovation are unavailable.

Two strands of technological development are notable for improving connectivity and openness. Improvements in data manipulation and visualization now allow firms to create genuinely useful "dashboards" to help their people see how they and the firm are performing. One of the most notable law firms in this respect is DWF, whose technology platform brings together a wealth of hard financial data with softer measures such as client feedback and personal objectives.

Alongside better presentation of data, firms are also using increasingly sophisticated social tools. Blogs and similar platforms have been used for some years, but these are now just one part of a range of methods for people to communicate about and reflect on their work and interests. Platforms like HighQ's Collaborate product provide opportunities for people to create content in blogs and wikis, but can also publish information automatically in the form of a Twitter-like activity stream to show what work is being done.

Improvements in connectivity and openness will improve the flow of information around the firm so that opportunities for innovation are much more visible than before. They can also improve the quality of collaboration on ideas. Firms will only see these benefits if people adapt to them and use them as part of their normal workflow.

Data dashboards are only useful if people act on what they see. Social platforms depend on genuine broad engagement; otherwise, they serve no purpose other than to amplify a few loud voices. Successful use of tools like these therefore depends on high levels of trust across the firm. The systems themselves need to be trustworthy, and people need to trust that the information they volunteer will not be misused by others. That kind of trust takes time to build if it isn't present already. Firms that already have high levels of trust will be able to develop their knowledge capability much faster as a consequence.

The prospect for knowledge capability and innovation in law firms

This account of the future may seem unattainable, even bleak. How can firms feel confident enough to move from traditional KM to a higher potential, but risky, knowledge capability approach? In fact, there are two key factors that may make it easier for law firms than for some other organizations to develop the right connectivity, openness, and trust to allow deeper knowledge capability to develop.

Unlike many commercial organizations, law firms tend to have a very clear focus. They help clients with the law. They don't often dilute that aim with services that are remote from the law, and the aim itself is well understood across the firm (not just by lawyers). Law firms also tend not to be very large. Very few contain more than 2-3,000 people. The combination of clarity of purpose and smallish size provides good conditions for trust to develop. With high levels of trust, better connectivity and openness facilitated by the right technical tools is more likely to be successful.

The second key factor for many law firms is the presence of professional support lawyers (PSLs) who can act as catalysts for optimum use of new tools and processes. While PSLs were initially recruited to take care of traditional KM activities, it would be a mistake to think that their role has stayed the same for the past 20-30 years. In fact, many PSLs already act as connectors between lawyers and other professionals across their firms. They stimulate the development of new products and services, and they often play important roles in teams making transformative changes in client service delivery and internal operations. In firms that have yet to make such changes, many PSLs are role models for the kind of trust and openness that firms need more widely. They also tend to be much more aware of the possibilities for change than many others in the firm.

Good innovation comes from a broad perspective on the world, an openness to novel insights and influences, reliable access to knowledge and insights across the firm (and from outside – clients and suppliers), and an organizational expectation that these should all come together coherently. That demands forward-looking knowledge activities, and PSLs are well placed to drive such work. Unlike their PSLs, most firms are only slowly waking up to the possibilities presented by a more forward-looking approach to understanding and developing their knowledge.

Whatever technologies or processes they choose, firms that actively pool and use the knowledge that all their people have – of their clients and their markets, of the legal market, of legal change on the horizon, and of the capabilities and limitations of the firm itself – are much more likely to be able to develop a coherent strategic response to the challenges they face. That response will inevitably be innovative, but it will also be impossible without the right knowledge capability.

Chapter 8:

Technology and the client relationship – moving to a new paradigm

By J Stephen Poor, chair emeritus, Seyfarth Shaw

The role of emerging technologies in the practice of law is the subject of much discussion – in particular, how technology will change large firm corporate law. Some argue that we stand on the cusp of transformation – that technology will soon completely displace humans.[1] Others argue that such talk is pure hype and that technology will merely continue to affect the way work product is produced, but not fundamentally change the way law is practiced. The premise of this chapter is that emerging technologies will not completely displace humans, but provide the possibility of reframing the client relationship in a way previously unknown to the industry. As that relationship is reframed, the client will experience the delivery of legal services differently through an alternate combination of technology delivery and human insight.

As a starting point, the question is, what do we mean by a "client relationship" and, by extension, the desired client experience? At one point in history, the practice of law, even in the largest law firms, was a craft. Perhaps better stated, a guild. Guild, in this sense, means a profession based almost exclusively on personal relationships. Lawyers essentially learned their craft through personal apprenticeships.[2] Lawyers earned business based largely on personal relationships with clients. Competition between firms existed but was genteel. The economics of the practice were largely left to the side, with the assumption that, if one excelled in one's craft, the business would take care of itself.

Over the past few decades, BigLaw practice has ceased to be a guild. It is now a business, and client relationships are run as a business – on both sides of the equation. Certainly, personal relationships continue to play a role in the profession. Economics, however, drive the decision-making. Business is earned and lost through competitive bid processes. The apprenticeship nature of the profession is quickly disappearing. Law firm lobbies may still contain high-backed leather chairs, but behind the façade is an industry focused on the bottom-line and driven by economics. The client experience now is largely one of vendor–vendee – cost, billing rates, and selection of providers are key variables.

This evolution is the result of many factors. The changes in the industry have been driven largely by the impact of the recession of 2007-08. In-house legal departments have grown dramatically as buyers work to reduce the cost of legal services. In addition, the past 15 years have seen a significant rise in competition from alternative sources – legal outsourcing, off-shore providers of legal services, pure legal technology companies and the like.[3] Nevertheless, while much of this is driven by economic factors, the change would not be possible without deployment of technology.

Competing forces in law firm evolution

In turn, the tale of the role of technology in this evolution is largely the story of two competing forces. The first is the inexorable advance of technology as a general matter. Computers, in all their glorious manifestations, have dramatically transformed the business landscape over the past few decades. The pace of that change is only accelerating. This means that new generations of lawyers entering the workforce are more native to the use of technology and have higher expectations for its deployment. Similarly, businesses – the purchasers of legal services – continue to take advantage of advances in technology to move forward, and expect the same from their counsel. Both, therefore, put pressure on firms and legal departments to adapt and use technological advances.

This inexorable advance of technology, however, runs into the second competing force – lawyers' resistance to change.[4] That resistance to change is remarkable. Lawyers hold tight to the notion of the practice of law as an art form. This resistance has and will slow the impact of technology developments, but it has not and will not stop it. As BigLaw loses its guild status, the potential business advantages from the deployment of technology ultimately overcome lawyer resistance.

Three decades ago, law firms had room after room filled with boxes of documents to be reviewed for law suits or pending corporate deals, and plenty of associates and paralegals billing by the hour to do the review. Firms had significant space set aside for law libraries full of people and books. Secretaries had only recently stopped using carbon paper, and "cut and paste" meant using scissors and tape. Many secretaries still took dictation or worked from handwritten documents to type legal documents. In fact, often, the secretary was the one responsible for ensuring that the form of the document met the particular filing requirements of the court. Once completed, pleadings in cases were filed by hand. Many was the time when a staff member was put on a plane to get a pleading filed in a distant court when time was of the essence. Failure to meet any of these obstacles raised potential malpractice concerns.

This all meant that the client experienced a very personal relationship. Lawyers tended to know their clients personally and the connection between the individuals often ran deep. Moreover, legal assistants tended to know the clients, and would spend time working around their particular needs. This led to a very individualized experience for the client. In turn, clients tended to stay loyal to their lawyers/friends. Putting work out to bid, or looking for different service delivery platforms, was rare indeed.

This firm and the underlying client relationship it created would be unrecognizable to attorneys entering the practice today. Attorneys typically draft and edit their own documents. Formatting is performed by the computer system. Document filing and trial presentations are largely done electronically. Document review – whether for deals or for law suits – is predominately handled through technology-based review or outsourced to vendors. Large teams of lawyers and paraprofessionals focused on document review no longer fill law firm hallways. As users become more sophisticated in their use of technology, the need for support functions has declined. Legal secretaries are fewer and farther between – a typical ratio now in BigLaw is five lawyers to one secretary. This, in turn, feeds into the de-personalization of the client/attorney relationship. The experience is now of businesses working with one another rather than individual professionals building a unique relationship.

So how did we get here and where are we going? Putting aside the use of technology in the functions of the practice that are not unique to the practice of law, such as accounting, finance, marketing and the like, the impact of technology on the core components of a law practice has been transformative. Over the past 30 years, we have seen three main phases of technology application and are at the cusp of a fourth, potentially more disruptive, phase.

Phase one: Information retrieval and processing

The first phase centered on technology around the retrieval and processing of information. In other words, the methods by which lawyers found information necessary to provide advice and the way in which that advice was processed by staff and team members. For example, the first Lexis terminal, which allowed for electronic search and retrieval of case law, was introduced in 1973. At the same time, and continuing throughout the 1980s, typewriters became increasingly sophisticated.

Ultimately, typewriters evolved into word processing systems, which resulted in the centralization of information processing. In turn, the word processing systems evolved into personal computers, resulting in the decentralization of information processing. An entire dissertation could be written on the impact of this change on intra-firm personal relationships.

On a macro level, however, this evolution had a variety of implications for the operations of law firms. These changes sped up the delivery of legal services in a way that was unheard of previously. While subsequent advances in technology make this moment seem quaint by comparison, the implications at the time were significant. Clients came to expect faster turnaround times and more efficient handling of documents and research. Interestingly, however, the inverse occurred. Rather than driving more efficiency, these technologies created more work – more documents to review, more revisions, more research, etc. Thus, this phase of computer deployment did much to enable law firms to operate more efficiently internally but did not fundamentally change how legal advice was delivered or the nature of the client relationship. Nor did they improve the quality of the product being delivered or drive material change in the way the client experienced legal services delivery.

Phase two: Connectivity

The second phase centers around the interconnectivity between lawyers and between lawyers and clients as a result of increasingly powerful machines. As the practice moved from the 1980s through the 1990s, several things happened – computer systems became connected through local and wide-area networks, email and internet connectivity became predominate factors in the way in which the practice was organized, and laptop computers began to replace desktop systems. As a result, lawyers and their clients became increasingly connected through technology.

The changes had significant ramifications for the way in which a law practice was organized. On one level, this meant that the mechanics of communication between lawyers and between lawyers and clients changed. Electronic communication began to substitute for telephonic communication or in-person discussions. Similarly, the speed of communication increased dramatically – clients expected virtually instantaneous responses to their questions. As noted above, this, in turn, began a change in the nature of the relationship between law firms and their clients. Exacerbated by economic drivers, the relationship between buyers of legal services and providers transformed from one based predominately on personal relationships to more of a vendor relationship. This, of course, does not necessarily mean that the client experience suffered – but it certainly changed in nature.

Phase three: Tools to empower the practice

These two phases of technology deployment facilitated the transition of the profession to an industry, and hastened the movement of the firm/client relationship to one based on economic factors. Building on the foundation created in the first two phases, in the third phase BigLaw began to use technology to empower lawyers in the practice. In other words, new tools became available that started to change the actual practice of law. Of course, the era of mobile devices freed lawyers almost completely from their desks while shackling them to their computers (in the form of the phone in their hands). At the same time, as software moved to the cloud and became more transparent, the ability of technology applications to enhance the productivity of lawyers began to predominate. Technology-assisted review of documents – whether in due diligence or discovery proceedings – has become widely accepted. These and other programs changed the nature of the work performed by law firms.

An example is the rise of technology coupling legal logic with document production. On the consumer front, the best example is LegalZoom (Rocket Lawyer is another). LegalZoom was founded in 2001 and was one of the first online providers to the public of basic legal documents, such as wills, incorporation documents and the like. Sitting in front of a computer screen, the user is guided through a series of on-screen questions until ultimately a legal document, such as a will, is produced. While human lawyers may be involved in some stage of the process, it is equally likely that the work will be produced without the need to interact with a live lawyer. This, of course, is a mixed blessing for the user of the services. It is cheaper and virtually on-demand. It lacks, however, the nuance of human delivery.

Referred to as "expert systems", this use of technology continues to break down the traditional notion of the law as a guild and a professional craft. Expert systems are difficult to build – requiring coding of the logic behind various legal principles or statutory framework. Once built, however, they are inexpensive to operate and require little human interaction. Thus, traditional rules governing the practice have less relevance.

In large part, the application of this technology has remained confined to the individual consumer or small business sector rather than the industry as a whole. It has done so primarily because of the desire of

BigLaw to cling to a business model that has worked well to date. Until this point, the legal industry has been able to deploy new technologies and still maintain its core business model – scale, hourly billing, and reliance on rates to drive profitability. The question is whether, in the face of emerging technologies, it can continue to do so.

Phase four: Emerging uses of technology and the client relationship

Given economic pressures and the nature of emerging technologies, logic dictates that the legal industry is on the cusp of significant change. The impact of the recession of 2007/08 changed the nature of the industry and, ten years on, we see the results.[5] Prior to that moment, demand for legal services was increasing every year. It was a seller's market. There was simply no pressure to change a business model that worked. With the recession, that dynamic changed. Since that period, demand for legal services has been either flat or declining. It is now a buyer's market, and they are looking at both cost and levels of value, i.e. customer service. That means law firms are in intense competition for business and face more pricing pressure. In turn, this means that they face pressure on the margins of the business while needing to meet the increased expectations of client service.

Most industries rely on technological improvements to deal with such economic realities, and such is the opportunity now presented to the legal industry. We are at the beginning of the current phase, which is the use of technology to replace humans in a variety of tasks associated with the delivery of legal services. Much has been written about so-called "robot lawyers" and "artificial intelligence" completely replacing lawyers. While pure artificial intelligence is not within reach, technologies such as robotic process automation, cognitive computing, and machine learning are enabling computers to perform many of the tasks formerly performed by humans.

In the legal industry, McKinsey Global Institute projects that 23 percent of tasks performed by lawyers could be automated with current technology.[6] What this means is that technology currently provides the ability to replace a significant portion of the work performed by lawyers with machines. In the context of contract management, for example, this means the ability of the machine to review thousands of contracts, look for provisions that create risk or are otherwise non-conforming, prepare alternative language, and serve it up to the user in an intuitive, understandable format. These, and other applications, create an opportunity to transform the way law is practiced. As discussed below, it allows technology to augment humans, giving attorneys the ability to focus on the human aspects of the craft.

Instructive in this regard are the examples of other professions. Accenture, for example, is ranked as one of the leaders in the deployment of robotic process automation.[7] At a recent conference on AI applications, an Accenture executive pointed out that five percent of Accenture's workforce is no longer human. If five percent does not sound like much, note that at Accenture, this equates to 20,000 full-time-equivalent positions. These are not projected numbers. This is current state. This is the potential of AI, and that potential is being tapped everywhere.

Magellan Health utilizes a suite of programs – all under the banner of artificial intelligence – to handle a significant portion of its process for reviewing and approving requests for medical tests. Robot reporters are on the rise in journalism, including the Associated Press's announcement in 2016 that an automated writing service will begin covering 10,000 minor league baseball games annually. Similarly, in 2016, semi-autonomous trucks completed the first European Truck Platooning Challenge, driving from various starting points across the EU to meet in Rotterdam.

To date, these developments have generated more discussion in the legal industry than actual adoption. In fact, with a few notable exceptions, the legal industry appears to be stuck in its historic patterns. In response to a flat market and rising expenses, the general response of the industry is to hire more lawyers and increase rates. This worked in the rising demand market of 2005. Perhaps firms are counting on an uptick in demand and a return to those days. Perhaps, with a radically different regime in Washington, regulatory change will even produce a short-term uptick. Nevertheless, as noted previously, the nature of the industry has fundamentally changed since 2008. In a world of flat or declining demand for the services of BigLaw, the reliance on rate increases to support profit growth is not a sustainable path for most firms.

So, what *exactly* is it that companies like Magellan Health, Accenture, and others know that the legal industry ignores? They know that, to compete and continue to survive, they cannot continue to operate in the same way. They know that it is essential to re-examine their business processes and continually redesign those processes to add value while removing cost. As they look at the changing need of the customers, juxtaposed with the business challenges they face, they recognize that current technologies can be a part of that redesign.

Take the example of Magellan Health. According to David Hodges, its chief medical officer, Magellan understood the need to redesign its process for reviewing and approving requests for medical tests.[8] The business problem included two variables – the need to reduce costs and eliminate unnecessary medical tests on the one hand, and the lack of tolerance for error on the other. Magellan used a combination of natural language processing, machine learning, and predictive analytics. And, yes, it made a sizeable monetary investment (which, it asserts, has produced a return on the investment).

Using technology to make good lawyers great

The question is whether the reluctance of lawyers to change can withstand the onslaught from the current phase of technology. Currently, BigLaw business is failing to use technology that is already available – technology that can make a significant difference in the way the industry operates. Magellan's articulated goal was to make "average" doctors into "great" doctors and to make "great" doctors even better. They will tell you they achieved this goal. This involved more than simply buying computer applications. It meant understanding what makes a doctor great, the process involved, and the intersection between human intelligence and the augmentation that can be provided by machines.

The same result will ultimately prevail in the legal industry. Technology has already facilitated change in the way in which the business operates, the way in which lawyers interact with each other and learn their craft, and the nature of the relationship between law firms and their clients, among others. In each stage, lawyer resistance delayed the adoption of technology longer than business logic would dictate. The current lag in adoption, therefore, is not a new development. Ultimately, however, the potential of emerging technologies is too important to ignore. Over the next few years, the industry will have the opportunity to embrace the power of technology to change the core nature of the delivery of legal services.

This presents an opportunity to rethink the nature of the client relationship. Nothing will reverse many of the trends toward cost control and redesign of the legal supply chain. At the same time, when asked about factors driving the hiring of counsel, purchasers of legal services tend to talk about value and legal expertise. Instead of focusing on those pillars, over the years, BigLaw has associated the notion of serving as a lawyer with tasks – document review, legal research, and on and on. In fact, this increasingly broad notion that certain tasks should be performed by lawyers has been among the variables fueling growth in the industry.

The peeling off of tasks by technology challenges this broad notion. Because of the impact of technology, we should no longer look at the client relationship with a recitation of tasks that make up the job of being a "lawyer". Instead, we have the opportunity to refocus on the quintessentially human characteristics – insight, relationships, empathy, the ability to see connections – at the core of the profession. It is not about finding the case; increasingly, technology can perform that task. It is about understanding and applying the case. It is not about reviewing the documents; other services can handle that responsibility faster and more effectively. It is about synthesizing the meaning of the document with the business terms of the deal. In essence, it is about enhancing the human elements to provide the highest level of client experience.

These quintessentially human traits are more important than ever. As clients find different ways to have legal services delivered, the need for people to operate at the edges of complexity becomes critical. The reality, however, is that this more traditional notion of lawyer as "trusted advisor" is essential. But the impact of technological advances creates an additional dimension. Client demands continue to change, and require a different way of thinking about the delivery of legal services. To succeed in meeting changing client demands, a lawyer must be able to manage and relate to the variety of alternative services available and be able to successfully use those capabilities to solve the problems facing clients. For example, we need to understand technology and how it can be used to augment the ability of people to deliver legal services. We need to understand the roles filled by alternative service providers or other allied professionals and how they fit into the solution set.

As we peel off tasks from lawyers, we need to look at the business problem from the clients' perspective – not the firm's perspective – and understand how to design solutions that solve those problems. Clients are looking for that combination of cost, speed of delivery and, where appropriate, a deep level of human insight. The organizations that are able to harness the power of technology to augment the strength of their people will be in a better position to deliver this client experience. In turn, in an increasingly competitive environment, this will lead to deeper and longer-lasting client relationships. This, of course, is the key to ultimate financial success.

References

1. See, e.g., Oliver Goodenough, "Legal Technology 3.0", Huffington Post, 6 April 2015; Richard Susskind, *Tomorrow's Lawyers: An Introduction to Your Future* (2013); Mark McKamey, *Legal Technology: Artificial Intelligence and the Future of Law Practice* (2017), 22 Appeal 45.
2. David Maister has written extensively on this topic, including the classic book, *The Trusted Advisor* (2000).

3. See, e.g., *Report on the State of the Legal Profession 2017*, Georgetown Center for the Legal Profession.
4. For interesting discussions of lawyer personality types, see the works of Dr. Larry Richard, including *The Lawyer Types*, *ABA Journal* (July 1993) and his writings at lawyerbrain.com.
5. *2018 Report on the State of the Legal Profession*, Georgetown Law School Center for the Legal Profession and Thomson Reuters Legal Executive Institute.
6. *A Future that Works: Automation, Employment and Productivity;* McKinsey Global Institute (2017).
7. 2016 HfS RPA Premier League Table for Transformative Enablers.
8. "'AI Solutions Optimize Doctors' Performance Says Magellan Health", AIBusiness.org (December 9, 2016).

Chapter 9:
Evolve *and* innovate – how to manage change in order to keep reward strategies fit for purpose

By Simon Nash, director, Insight Limited and formerly global HR director at Carey Olsen

It is an often unsettling realization for ambitious new managing partners to discover that the very competencies that brought them success as high-performing lawyers in the first part of their careers are in many cases incompatible, and even opposite to, the skills and mental models that their firm needs them to master and deliver now. What's more, in these past two decades, the length of the "honeymoon period"[1] to acquire and perfect these skills has become radically diminished, as firms are pressured to produce excellent results quarter-on-quarter, just to maintain position.

Whether you are a managing partner or an executive board member responsible for people and performance, or a human resources professional in a professional services firm, or even a reward consultant delivering advisory services into law firms, this chapter seeks to outline some of the new thinking required and some of the new tools that are becoming available to help firms survive into the next decade. Specifically we apply this thinking to the issue of lawyers' compensation, although it will be obvious that the same analysis applies to every aspect of practice management.

Now is the time for new thinking, new technology, and new reward practices for professional services firms. In this context, the way firms master new ways of thinking about business and change will enable them to achieve the laser-like focus and market differentiation that will give them the edge in the "People and Performance Equation".[2]

So what are these competencies? Broadly speaking, we can define three key areas that will make a good deal of the difference. These are data analytics, predictive modelling, and change dynamics. Naturally, many readers will feel that several dimensions of critical importance have been left out of this list. Where are the skills relating to client care, matter management, people communications, knowledge curation, and financial administration? Well, of course these are still important, but to a greater degree than ever before they are not *differentiating*. Many firms have tightened the slack in all of these areas and have also installed technologies to extract what additional value there was in the firm's value chain. A differentiating factor is one that (a) makes an appreciable difference to the firm's performance in one or more of the key metrics of margin, pricing, utilization, or leverage, and (b) does that in a way that cannot be instantly replicated across the market of competing firms.

We will examine these three factors separately, and then we will show, in two case studies, how they can come together into a differentiating approach to law firm reward. Before we continue, however, it's worth attending up front to one common objection to this approach. Many of the firms that are most resistant to this breaking wave of change are those that have enjoyed, and are continuing to experience, a long run of success. "The old model has brought us financial success, reputational prestige, and an unassailable position, so why change?"

While it is indeed true that some of the factors highlighted below were not available to firms during their golden years, it is equally true that the firms that will achieve market dominance in the next generation are already investing heavily in these areas, and doing so without the deadweight of legacy practices to deal with.

Data analytics

What is data analytics? The first problem we encounter in this new wild west of organizational innovation is that every software vendor, business school academic, or futurist has slightly different nomenclature and definitions for what are roughly the same things. Here we use data analytics to describe an approach to understanding your business in its present and recent past, through the thorough examination of very large data sets. Data analytics includes work done under the headings of business intelligence (BI), and online reporting and analytical processing (OLAP). It often relies on more fundamental concepts such as data warehousing, real-time analytics, cloud computing, and quantitative benchmarking.

Data analytics practitioners have two principal methodologies; EDA and CDA (exploratory and confirmatory data analysis). EDA seeks to find patterns and relationships in the data, while CDA applies statistical techniques to determine whether a hypothesis is valid or false. You could think of them as a detective and a judge.[3]

In law firm reward terms, the practice of data analytics has lots to offer. Firms have for a very long time sought to make reward decisions, such as pay reviews, bonus awards, and profit share allocations on a rational and business-like basis. But this desire has been hampered by the lack of genuinely robust data and statistically sound methods for interpreting them, as well as a generally poor grasp of the psychology of motivation and some unhelpful home-spun philosophies of management. It is only in recent years that firms have access to the kind of computing power and statistical expertise, often coded into smart applications, that is required to perform the kind of analyses that deliver profound insights into the real drivers of value in the firm and the people and performance leading indicators of such value.

What's more, this level of analytics is not just available in respect of the numbers inside the firm. The field of data benchmarking has also gone through its renaissance and now there are emerging some very smart service providers using "big data" processing tools and cloud technology, that are close to being able to promise the ability to "compare anything with anyone".[4] If it is true that "information is the oil of the 21st century, and analytics is the combustion engine,"[5] then perhaps it is time for law firms to leave behind the trusted pony-and-cart approach to practice economics.

Predictive modelling

Just as with data analytics, there is an even wider range of terms in use to describe the future-oriented mapping of scenarios to develop an understanding of how the complex data concerning people and markets are likely to change given a variety of different environmental variables and management decisions, which we will here refer to as predictive modelling. The model created from the data may be a simple linear equation or a complex neural network, composed of algorithms run on sophisticated software.

The key points to take on board are these. Firstly, while scenario planning has its roots in the business schools and top corporate boardrooms of the 1970s, it has now come of age as being accessible, relevant, and affordable to businesses of virtually any scale. Secondly, the field has undergone its own technology-led revolution. Now that it is relatively straightforward to get so many of the firm's metrics into a cloud database or physical server, it becomes possible to run models over the firm's own data, rather than using elaborately constructed artificial replicas of a "typical" firm. This gives greater accuracy and credibility to the exercise. Thirdly, the increase in computing power has enabled scenarios to be tweaked and tested in real time. The opportunity to play out scenarios immediately can make law firm strategy sessions a much more dynamic and engaging process.

Further developments in the field will make predictive analytics even better, as new technology businesses seek to harness the power of machine learning (often misnamed "artificial intelligence") to improve the models' correspondence to reality over time, giving greater predictive validity and strategic utility.

Change dynamics

Change dynamics is a field that attempts to describe the process of change in organizational, psychological, and systemic terms. It seeks, as with the previous two methodologies, to use data scientifically to describe what actually goes on in firms, rather than using management theory, or worse, an oral tradition of common sense maxims to prescribe what ought to be going on. The premise of change dynamics is that if leaders really understand how change actually takes place, in individuals and businesses, they will be better equipped to manage change better for sound organizational outcomes. "Typically the HR department doesn't have analytics experience and the analytics experts don't have HR experience. That's why change management is critical to HR analytics success."[6]

One classic insight from the field of change dynamics is Professor Michael Kirton's Adaption-Innovation theory.[7] Kirton hypothesised that when it comes to change some people think principally in terms of gradual improvements to what currently exists (whom he called the "Adaptors"), while others think principally in terms of inventing something new to replace what is in use (his "Innovators"). This pioneering work established that the degree to which a person was more adaptive or innovative was highly constant through life. Researchers using this finding have also discovered some statistically valid tendencies between people of different professions.

It may not surprise readers to learn that the legal profession has an extremely high preponderance of adaptors and adaptive thinking. Law firms, therefore, have relatively few innovators and an environment typically unreceptive to innovative ideas. Whether this is a result of self-selection – adaptive personalities think they will enjoy the life of a lawyer and therefore embark on JD/LLB courses in greater number, or a result of systemic selection – the innovative personalities do not survive the environment of legal supervision and training in such great numbers as their adaptive peers, it is not possible to say.[8]

Whatever its cause, leaders of law firms have to deal with the effect. Law firms need to appreciate that the dominant mode of thinking around the partnership table is one of incrementalism, of Fabian gradualism, or small-c conservatism. Lawyers' respect for traditions and precedents should not really be too much of a surprise in the common law world of *stare decisis*. As a result, innovation can be hard, as strange sounding ideas will be deeply resisted without the participants really knowing why.

The following two case studies demonstrate how two different firms have navigated this new world of big data and innovative change, and have done so with great results.

Case study one – using analytics to remodel contingent reward

A law firm – which for the purposes of this chapter shall be referred to as Gage Whitney Pace[9] LLP (GWP) – wished to revise its approach to contingent reward. The first thing it needed to do was to bring some expert analysis to bear. Data was sought and analyzed to address a series of paradigmatic questions. What does the firm do now? What effects does this have on people and performance outcomes? What do its competitors for talent in the local market do, and with what results? These research questions were posed both in the specific area of contingent reward and also in a total reward context. The analyses sought to examine these questions both in terms of raw financial/statistical data and also in terms of the psychological messages that were received by the associate population.

So what did the internal data show? Gage Whitney's prior system of contingent reward was highly discretionary, and both the decision-making process and the outcomes were veiled in secrecy. This exacerbated the low level of trust in GWP's reward systems among associates and probably contributed to its higher than average levels of unforced leavers who went straight to competing local firms.

The external study of contingent reward in the local market was telling. The other firms all had a approach to contingent reward that was highly similar to each other. You could not, from the raw data, really tell one firm from another. This is not unusual in professional services firms – which tend to huddle around the security of common approaches, even when they desire to have different results.

Two yardstick metrics for comparing contingent reward schemes are incidence and spread. Incidence measures, on average, the proportion of eligible employees who receive a bonus against those who don't. In the case of GWP's direct competitors, all had an incidence score of between 92 and 96 percent. This meant that approximately the top 95 percent of associates were awarded a performance bonus and only the bottom five percent were not.

Spread, in contingent reward, measures the degree to which the bonuses of the very best performers differ from those of the average and also the very worst. In the study, all of the top four local competitors were shown to have a spread of between six and nine percent of salary, with a statistically normal distribution of awards within this narrow range. So what was the message to associates which was encoded into the designs of these schemes? The incidence figure said "We are all in this together," so everyone gets something, and the spread said "Your contributions are all pretty equivalent," so no one gets particularly much more than anyone else.

Looking at the data, Gage Whitney had two initial options. Either, it could design a scheme that delivered similar outcomes to the rest of the market, which would thereby take contingent reward off the table as a non-comparable factor, or it could seize the initiative and design a scheme with radically different outcomes that encoded for very different employee communications messages. To explore this more fully, a number of rule schemes were designed, and these potential new solutions were financially modelled in great detail under a number of stress conditions.

The design settled for was radically different in both structure and outcomes. On the measure of incidence, GWP decided to create a scheme that targeted around 55 percent of associates as meriting a bonus, and therefore around 45 percent would not. This design is easily translated by the employee base as saying, "Not all of you are doing enough or are good enough, and only those who are delivering superior performance will get a bonus on top of their core reward package". Quite a different message in content and tone!

The firm also decided to use the budget saved by not giving bonuses to the lower half of the population to enhance the spread. Rather than a six to nine percent spread, the firm adopted a five to 20 percent spread. This clearly communicated the message that "Elite performers will be rewarded superlatively here".

These two design features alone had the potential effect of pouring aviation fuel on the summer barbecue, but the firm was advised to go even further with some more bold design features which would enhance the difference between the new scheme and anything else in the market.

For a start, Gage Whitney adopted a "single measure" performance metric. This is often regarded as a highly risky strategy, as single measure schemes can often be gamed for sub-optimal advantage. To avoid this, many firms create very complex multi-measure schemes, often with annual changes in scheme rules to outlaw the abuses and failures of the previous year. For GWP, the particular single measure was wisely chosen. It was a factor highly correlated to the financial success of the firm, one ultimately in the control of the clients, rather than the associates or partners, and one which all associates could monitor on a daily basis if they so chose.

What did this say to the employee population? Well, it communicated that by acting transparently the firm was treating them as adults in business, whose interests were directly aligned with those of the firm and its clients. It also said that extremes of high effort or ability could correlate to extremes of reward not available in the other firms in the market. In one stroke the message went out both to the employees of GWP and also to all those in its competitors that, "If you are a mediocre performer you'll be better off in one of the other firms, but if you are an elite performer, your efforts will be rewarded more at Gage Whitney".

What does this case study show? Firstly, one should not underestimate the importance of data. The radical proposal could only be made in the context of a sound analysis of the market context and some sophisticated modelling of the cost parameters of the scheme. Beyond data, there is a psychological angle too. All business processes have an explicit and implicit message to the employee population. Often these are at odds with each other, and sometimes contrast sharply with the explicit employee communications of the firm. Naturally, intelligent employees decode the implicit message and quickly discount any explicit messaging as corporate propaganda. In the GWP scheme, the embedded values of the scheme were crafted so as to create a disruptive difference in the local market, and one that would have impacts into other areas of people management.

Its effects were stunning and led to dramatic growth in fee income, talent attractiveness, and the growth of the firm. As a coda to the story it is interesting that after nearly a decade, not only has the firm maintained the scheme design virtually unchanged, but many local competitors have also adjusted their schemes to defend talent.

Case study two – using business model innovation to solve supply and demand fluctuations

This law firm – which for similar reasons will be called McKenzie Brackman[10] (MB) – was facing two problems at the same time. One was quite a nice problem to have, and the other was not regarded as a problem, but more a feature of the environment, until a more radical approach to the people and performance equation was pioneered.

To lift the veil, the first "problem" was that Mackenzie Brackman was very successful at attracting clients and more new work from existing clients.

Law firms experience this fluctuation in demand for their services at both the level of the economic cycle – a booming economy generates more corporate work and the other side of the economy keeps the litigators and insolvency practitioners busy – and also within a market with respect to competitive market share.

Law firms typically have sought to cope with these two factors by a resourcing-led strategy – hire more trainees and be more active in the lateral market during the boom, and make redundancies and lay-offs during hard times. The problem with this has always been that law firms are typically hopeless at judging the labour market supply at one end of the long pipeline, to balance legal service demand at the other. Reward policy has been a reactive servant of this resourcing-led strategy – by making the firm more attractive in talent markets through extravagant job offers, which often cause employee relations problems further down the road.

Mackenzie Brackman was in just this position of gaining market share in a rising market, just at the time of a talent shortage. So all firms in the local market were seeking to hire the same lawyers at the same time, which is usually a recipe for unsustainable compensation inflation and margin pressure.

The advice received was to look at the issue more holistically. Mackenzie Brackman had traditionally conceived of its office as the place where work happened and of full-time professional lawyers as the people who did the work. Part-time workers were regarded as minor exceptions to the rule and atypical. For the partners, all of whom had had conventional full-time legal careers, the equations between hours of work, rates of pay, billable hours, and headcount in the office were all pretty fixed. But the people and performance equation teaches us that these are not fixed coefficients, but rather they are ratios. This means that legal work can be profitable for the firm, valuable for the client, and worthwhile for the lawyer in many different geometries.

So how did Mackenzie Brackman utilize this insight to solve the inefficiencies of fluctuations of talent supply and client demand? Well, they sought in many ways to engage or re-engage parts of the talent market who would not be interested in coming to the office for a 0800-1900, Monday to Friday, working week. When a facilitator brainstormed the issue with them, they were surprised that there were many more solutions than they could have guessed. Retirees were a good example. The recently retired did not have the appetite or energy to resume a permanent job, but could quite happily do bits and pieces of work at home during times of peak demand. People taking study leave or career breaks presented similar opportunities. Parents who had ceased work for a period of time to focus on their families could similarly do a few hours flexibly. Likewise employees who had relocated away from the firm's locations to follow their spouse's career. The list seemed practically endless. Each category brought issues of scheduling, supervision, insurance, contractual terms and the like, but those are all fairly easy problems to solve. The more interesting problem to solve was the remuneration issue.

Law firms, unlike Barrister's chambers in some jurisdictions, have traditionally regarded client fees and associate pay as quite separate decision processes. Once the firm has set these two financial variables the challenge is then to manage the engagement at an economic rate. Managing the financial risks of getting the work done for less than the fee quote and carrying the locked up working capital were what earned the firm its profit margin on the matter.

With this new motley gaggle of atypical outworkers there was no need to take the same approach. Why not offer discrete packets of work at a fixed fee and with a completion deadline, with payment after the work had been accepted and paid for by the firm's client? It was then up to the worker to decide how quickly or slowly to do the work, in line with their other life interests. MB would know it was going to make a margin on the job, and the firm's working capital was protected by not paying for work in advance as with conventional employment.

Naturally, there is nothing new in this model. The market between TV or theatre producers, talent agents and actors works in a mostly similar way. Parts of the publishing sector are also organized in this way. Yet for law firms, who traditionally find it easy to advise clients on novel and creative business solutions – but find it incredibly difficult to view their own business model as a simple set of variables that can be reconfigured – this was culturally very challenging.

In conclusion

We have seen that remuneration innovation may be thought of in two ways. You can gradually improve the present situation by small increments, or you can take a big leap into the unknown. For a variety of reasons, law firms often tended to prefer the former. The risks are generally perceived as smaller, but in fact they expose the firm to a more insidious risk of slipping behind the market imperceptibly slowly. In every generation there are one or two individual lawyers or firms in each market who redefine an area of practice with a bold paradigmatic change of the sort more commonly expected in sectors such as technology or investment banking. When those changes are successful they set the scene for the next phase of incrementalism within that new paradigm.

The challenge for 21st century PSF leaders is to discern when to be bold and when to be more careful, and in both cases how to achieve the benefits of change with fewer of the side effects. The way to mitigate the risk of this kind of innovation are through the application of three disciplines. Firstly, by taking a thoroughly scientific approach to the data. "Without data you are just another person with an opinion."[11] For lawyers taking a "big data" approach typically means using unfamiliar technologies. The second discipline requires being equally rigorous in the scientific basis of any psychological assumptions about the motivations of lawyers at work, both individually and as a system or culture. Transparency can be a big enabler of cultural change in the firm, as it enables a foundation of honest, adult-to-adult, communication between leaders and employees. The third is applying the methods of thinking that will bring creatively innovative and experimental options to the table.

All three of these require the investment in trusted advisors, who may well be people with specialist skillsets within the firm, working alongside experts in the application of data, psychology, and thinking. The chilling prophecy of W. E. Deming is as true now as ever: "It is not necessary to change. Survival is not mandatory."[12]

References

1. Nick Jarrett–Kerr (2009) *Strategy for Law Firms*. The Law Society.
2. An approach which may be found in Nash (2012) *Managing Partner*; Vol. 14, Issue 8; Vol. 14, Issue 10; Vol. 15, Issue 1 and Vol. 15, issue 2; largely inspired by Maister (1993) *Managing the Professional Service Firm*, Free Press, New York.
3. A distinction first drawn by legendary statistician, John W. Tukey, who coined the terms "bit" (of data) and "software", in his *Exploratory Data Analysis* (1977).
4. Mercer's Comptryx is a good large business example and ALX Analytix.com is an exciting start-up in this space targeting businesses with fewer than 2,500 employees.
5. Peter Sondergaard, Gartner Research.
6. Luke Marson, co-founder iXerv, "One Secret to a data driven HR Culture," January 2018.
7. A-I theory now has over 200 published articles and 70 doctoral theses.
8. Perhaps there is an interesting PhD here for a psychologist with an interest in legal practice.
9. Readers familiar with the fictional universe of Aaron Sorkin's drama will recognise the name of this firm.
10. I am indebted to Steven Bochco's entertaining legal drama of several decades ago for this name.
11. Attributed to W. E. Deming.
12. Cited in Frank Voehl (1995): *Deming The Way We Knew Him*. CRC Press.

Chapter 10:
Innovation as a business development strategy

By Scott Rechtschaffen, chief knowledge officer, Littler Mendelson

Law firm marketing approaches have evolved

Consider the marketing phrases that law firms have gone through in an effort to differentiate themselves from their competition. Once, law firm collateral, websites, and advertising focused on "great lawyering" – essentially, saying their attorneys were smarter and more skilled than attorneys at the other firms. Then, law firm marketing shifted to a focus on "partnering" and "collaborating" with clients – claiming their attorneys understood clients' business better than the attorneys at other firms. More recently, it seems to be about being "cost effective".

But, how exactly does a firm – say a firm ranked as number 76 on the AmLaw 100 list – demonstrate through its website or advertising copy that its attorneys are smarter, or that they are better client partners than, say, the attorneys at a firm ranked as AmLaw number 39, 79, or 86? With bios showing where its attorneys went to law school? With lists or anonymized case studies? Can law firms seriously market their advantage over competitors with claims of greater intellectual prowess or saying they are more cost effective? Saying so does not necessarily make these firms better value. Are these really the attributes that distinguish one law firm from another? Firms highlight their attorneys' knowledge of a client's business and its industry. It is impossible to be a great lawyer without that, but it's not a differentiator – it's table stakes.

In the past few years, many law firms have begun to focus their marketing and brand-building efforts on a tangible attribute to significantly differentiate themselves from the competition using "innovation". However, true "innovation" is more than a passing buzzword, or the marketing phrase of the moment. It is a strategy for improving the delivery of legal services and positively impacting the law firm-client relationship to the benefit of both. Innovation strategies include developing robust knowledge management programs, providing clients with comprehensive legal information offerings, implementing legal process management and legal process improvement methodologies, and deploying genuinely cutting-edge technology (i.e. beyond iPhone and Android apps, sophisticated websites, and extranets).

Why innovation is relevant for today's corporate legal clients

Developing an innovation strategy is much more than a marketing device because innovation, used this way, addresses the most critical demands that corporate legal clients are now making of their outside counsel. Since the Great Recession of 2008 and its impact on the legal industry, clients have increasingly demanded a change in the way their law firms deliver services. For most firms, the days of routine annual rate increases and ill-defined – or "blank check" – budgets for legal matters are a distant memory from the golden days of the legal industry. Now, clients demand reduced costs, increased efficiency, greater transparency, and higher quality standards. In-house counsel have greater leverage than ever to change the way their outside counsel deliver legal services. Corporate clients also have more options to get the legal resources they need. What many attorneys and law firms do not realize is that they are no longer just competing with other law firms; they are competing with Google and the vast array of resources that the web offers.

Today, an innovation strategy has to be much more than the technology "innovations" that law firms have adopted over the past decades – email, smartphones, online legal research, extranets, and e-filing. These have been sustainable innovations enabling lawyers to communicate and collaborate with their clients more efficiently, but they did not fundamentally change how legal services were delivered and by whom. The newly emerging technologies – for example, predictive coding, document automation, and "expert advisor" systems, such as Littler's ComplianceHR suite of products, discussed below – are disruptive technologies. Over time, they will vastly reduce the need for, respectively: attorney-performed document review; attorneys drafting routine documents; and attorneys answering basic client questions.

Legal services have largely remained a one-attorney-to-one-user interaction model (or a many-attorney-to-one-client model). But the rest of the world leverages technology on a one-provider-to-hundreds-or-thousands-of-users model. It is unreasonable to believe that lawyers will remain a unique coterie of professionals delivering bespoke services, while the rest of the world – including every other major profession – has moved further into the online mainstream. As legal industry prognosticator Richard Susskind has noted:

"It is simply inconceivable that information technology will radically alter all corners of our economy and society and yet somehow legal work will be exempt from any change."[1]

For innovation to become more than just a marketing phrase, for a law firm to truly establish its brand as an "innovative" law firm, it must develop and implement a strategy that truly transforms how legal services – legal information, litigation, advice and counseling, transactional work – are delivered. It is insufficient to simply "check the box" by launching one or two apps or adding more generic articles and news alerts to a firm's website. A true innovation strategy envisions dramatically and comprehensively changing the way firms interact with and serve their clients that helps clients make money, save money, look good, or sleep better. A successful innovation strategy cannot just change the game, it has to change it for the better.

Innovation at Littler

At Littler, we have spent the past two decades developing and implementing just such an innovation strategy. We began by offering clients a robust knowledge management program, with a content marketing strategy that delivered critical, valuable legal, business, and legislative insights in a way that other firms could seldom match. More recently, though, we have moved to develop technology tools, legal processes, and products that offer our clients alternatives to the traditional one-to-one client-attorney relationship and the billable hour model.

Through these efforts, Littler has become widely recognized as an innovative law firm – it has become a core component of our brand, if you will. Over the past few years we have been consistently recognized by major publications, and both the firm and our individual attorneys have received awards for innovation. Increasingly, we are hearing clients reference our investment in innovative service solutions as a differentiator.

The beginnings of innovation at Littler – Knowledge management

About 15 years ago, a number of major US law firms began adding knowledge management functions to their corporate infrastructure. Many hired chief knowledge officers or directors of knowledge management. Initially, the goal was to enhance access to the treasure trove of precedential work product that law firms seemingly generate in their sleep – model transactional documents, best practice forms and policies, pleadings and litigation documents, and advice memos. In those early days, knowledge management was designed to prevent lawyers from constantly re-inventing the wheel by providing them with access to the best work product already created by experienced colleagues within their firms. This would, of course, increase efficiency and save clients time and money.

Naturally, many firms turned to technology solutions. Often, knowledge management became an adjunct to the IT department and the leading advocates for knowledge management were those law firm partners who had a real passion for and fascination with technology. Firms developed and deployed expertise databases, enterprise search systems, and elaborate subject-matter intranets. Similarly, at Littler, our knowledge management program focused initially on providing the firm's attorneys with ready access to the enormous amount of precedential work product, and it eased access to the firm's subject matter experts.

We developed internal databases and collections of substantive materials. We deployed an enterprise search platform that enabled attorneys to quickly find the work product they needed to work more efficiently and avoid re-creating the wheel in serving their clients.

However, Littler realized that focusing knowledge management solely on improving internal attorney efficiency ignored the advantages that a robust knowledge management program could contribute to the firm's service to its clients, as well as the firm's brand and overall marketing efforts.

Knowledge management as the foundation of a comprehensive content marketing strategy

Recognizing the brand value and importance of truly leveraging firm-created content, Littler's knowledge management program began to focus extensively on creating and aggregating valuable substantive content in ways that informed clients of critical developments and demonstrated the firm's deep and broad subject matter expertise. This was a natural evolution of Littler's already heavy investment in content dissemination that demonstrated its substantive legal knowledge and analysis. Littler first published *The National Employer®* book before it had a single office outside of California – which naturally helped develop Littler's brand as a national law firm even before we were truly national in geographic scope. Similarly, Littler published its *Guide to International Employment and Labor Law* before it had a single office outside of the United States – again, helping to develop Littler's global brand before we had a presence in 14 countries, as we do today. In both instances, the smart development and distribution of content helped define Littler's brand, providing a natural base for our knowledge and expertise.

Initially, these knowledge management efforts included not only client conferences, client alerts, and newsletters, but also comprehensive compendiums with in-depth analysis of pertinent legal issues and developments. Some of these publications and content initiatives are as follows.

The *Employer Series* publications

Littler developed this print publication series over 30 years ago to be a comprehensive primer of employment and labor law. Initially, the *The National Employer®* book was created as a loose-leaf notebook designed to be handed out at client conferences. Over time, Littler developed relationships with major legal content publishers to transform that thin notebook into an exhaustive 6,000-plus page encyclopedia covering federal law and the law of over 30 states – published in both print and digitally. Today, it ranks as one of the most comprehensive compendiums of US employment and labor law.

Legal developments alerts

Littler typically publishes about 250 legal development alerts each year in various formats – as electronic newsletters, client alerts, and blog posts. These are sent directly to clients, posted on the firm's website, posted to social media sites, and distributed through various channels such as Mondaq, Lexology, JD Supra, and others. At one point, Littler maintained 11 separate blogs covering topics as diverse as workplace privacy, global employment law developments, global immigration, electronic discovery, and wage-hour law. (Littler's blogs have since been incorporated into Littler's overall content platform and no longer exist as traditional stand-alone blogs.)

White papers and Littler reports

Every year, Littler publishes in-depth white papers and reports covering major developments and coming trends in employment and labor law. Littler's *Annual Report on EEOC Developments* has been published annually for the past five years and provides a comprehensive examination of significant events and enforcement activities of the Equal Employment Opportunity Commission. Published in 2012, Littler's *"Bring Your Own Device" to Work Movement* report, co-authored by over 20 Littler attorneys, was a pioneering examination of the growing BYOD trend and its potential impact on employment law in the workplace. This Littler report helped enhance the reputation of Littler's burgeoning workplace privacy and data security practice group.

Single-subject publications

Littler has also worked with many of the major legal industry publishers on books dedicated to specific topics within the field of employment and labor law. Our attorneys have developed authoritative publications that enable us to say, truly, that "we wrote the book" on major subject areas of interest to our clients.[2]

Recently, the CEO of one of the leading online legal research platforms observed that, with its prolific output, Littler must surely rank as one of the top 10 leading producers of legal content in the US. He then asked how Littler was able to generate such a huge volume of content given that most attorneys are generally incentivized and compensated for generating client work, not writing books and white papers.

How do we do it?

There are really several answers to this question. First, with its long history of using content to market the firm's authoritative knowledge and expertise in the field of employment and labor law, it had become part of our firm culture that attorneys are expected to contribute to the firm's publishing efforts. Second, Littler has always stressed the importance of individual attorneys becoming "subject matters experts" in the many sub-domains that make up the field of employment and labor law. Attorneys who wish to develop business and new clients – and get referrals of business from within the firm – are encouraged to establish themselves in fields that are critical to our clients, such as privacy, employee benefits, executive compensation, and union-management relations. Writing and publishing on those topics is one of the best ways to do so.

Clearly, Littler's investment in building a substantial knowledge management (KM) department is one of its significant advantages and critical resources. Our KM department was established in 2001. Currently, Littler has over 15 dedicated knowledge management counsel (all attorneys with significant employment and labor experience). We have three dedicated research attorneys and over 15 professionals on our research and library team. All work together to generate a large amount of legal content that is valuable to our clients.

Within this larger group, we have a dedicated content publishing team that is responsible for producing initial drafts, reviewing content with attorney subject-matter experts, editing the content received from SMEs, and preparing and formatting content for publication. To ensure quality, most content generated by Littler attorneys is reviewed prior to publication by our publications review committee – a group consisting of knowledge management counsel and over 50 attorneys from across the firm, representing most of our major practice areas.

In addition to Littler's knowledge management department, the firm's client relations and marketing (CR&M) department plays an equally critical role in Littler's content marketing strategy. The CR&M team oversees the distribution of Littler's content through its numerous online channels, and manages the many content distribution relationships Littler maintains with third parties, whether they be subscribers or syndicators, and increasingly we are using data analytics to refine our content distribution strategies. The CR&M team is further leveraging Littler's content through an increasingly more robust social media and public relations strategy that takes full advantage of the brand-building opportunities social media provides.

Innovative legal service solutions as a brand differentiator for Littler

While a comprehensive content marketing program that provides clients and prospective clients with critical legal information plays an important role in a firm's innovation strategy, it is only one prong of a broader strategy. The firm must also demonstrate by its actions – as well as in its marketing – that it is committed to innovation, by being willing to change the way clients and lawyers work together.

About 10 years ago, Littler began taking its KM strategy to the next level. Using many of the same teams and enhanced content, we began building online tools – "service solutions" – that would give clients direct access to the firm's knowledge management and other useful resources. Our first major effort was Littler GPS®, an online subscription service that provided clients with access to a comprehensive database of multi-jurisdiction surveys – covering topics as diverse as minimum wage requirements or lactation accommodation obligations across every major US jurisdiction. Because employment law requirements are often state-specific, employers need to be aware of the various requirements across the jurisdictions in which they operate. Eventually, Littler GPS grew to cover over 65 employment law topics and included weekly updates of new legislative and regulatory developments in any jurisdiction.

Next, we began to provide online toolkits providing clients with access to information and resources covering specific industries and subject areas. For example, our Home Care Toolkit provides online compliance resources for employers in the home health care industry.

Our Littler X-celerator™ provides start-up companies with access to resources to help them keep their growing businesses compliant with federal and California employment laws. Littler HR PolicySmart™ is an online resource enabling any company to keep track of changes in legal requirements that might impact their HR policies and procedures.

More recently, Littler launched two of its most ambitious offerings – Littler CaseSmart® and ComplianceHR. Littler CaseSmart represents, in our view, the future of employment law. It is a completely re-imagined process for managing administrative charges, single-plaintiff litigation, and employment law class actions. It combines proprietary technology, an alternative staffing model, and a completely differentiated workflow process for handling legal matters. In the past five years we have handled over 12,000 administrative charges and almost 400 litigation matters using this process, providing our clients with significant cost savings as well as transparent access to matter management.

ComplianceHR is a unique joint venture between Littler and Neota Logic, a leading legal technology software provider. ComplianceHR's suite of products enable in-house counsel to efficiently handle routine requests from their internal HR and business unit clients, answering important but repetitive questions such as whether a given employee qualifies as overtime exempt or whether an individual can lawfully be engaged as an independent contractor. ComplianceHR also offers applications that generate routine documents such as employment agreements, NDAs, and non-competes.

Conclusion

These various initiatives represent Littler's effort to provide unique and innovative services to its clients, recognizing that many legal services will inevitably move to an online service delivery model; not overnight, but over time. We are attempting to emulate, and move with clients to, the web-based service delivery model that is now the norm in virtually every other industry.

Of course, we recognize that there will always be a need for a trusted advisor – lawyers who can work with clients to develop bespoke strategies and solutions, delivering premium advice and counseling. So, while we know that there are limits to the services that can be delivered to clients online, we strongly believe that being at the forefront of developing unique legal services in ways that can help our clients be more successful demonstrates a genuine commitment to client service.

It is also a reflection of our commitment to making innovation a key part of our brand.

References

1. Susskind, R., *Tomorrow's Lawyers: An Introduction to Your Future*, Oxford University Press, 2013.
2. These publications currently include, among others: *Littler Mendelson on Employment Law Class Actions* (LexisNexis, Third Edition); *Whistleblowing & Retaliation* (LexisNexis, 5th edition); *The Littler Mendelson Guide to International Employment & Labor Law* (LexisNexis, 4th edition); *Disability Discrimination and the Workplace* (BNA, 2nd edition); *Unfair Competition and Intellectual Property Protection in Employment Law: Contract Solutions and Litigation Guide* (BNA); *Wage and Hour Answer Book* (Wolters Kluwer Law & Business).

Chapter 11:
Are you your vendor's captive? How to optimize your research dollars

By Oz Benamram, chief knowledge officer, and Kathy Skinner, director of research and information services, White & Case

What do you do when one of your most longstanding and costly vendor relationships takes a dramatic turn for the worse? When your "preferred provider" no longer appears interested in offering their product to you at a price that reflects declining use and a growing number of alternatives in the market? When the relationship makes you feel like a hostage instead of a partner? That was our situation, and we are sharing our story in the hope that it will resonate with and help others.

It will come as no surprise to the law firm audience that the world of legal information has fundamentally changed in recent years. As the landscape of research tools continues to evolve in some exciting and useful ways, we need to continually reexamine past, well-reasoned choices and longstanding biases and make hard decisions about which resources stay and which ones go in our firms, driven by the ever-shifting tension between cost and benefit. Firms can no longer support expensive research resources that come with vendor-mandated requirements to purchase large sets of redundant content or enterprise-wide access that is neither needed nor desired. In addition, firms have strong incentives to free up budget for forward-looking tools with analytics and AI features that can anticipate future legal practice needs and are being developed and offered largely outside of the traditional research vendor realm.

These and other reasons compelled White & Case to forge a new and ongoing path toward optimizing our portfolio of research tools, driving toward a complement of unique research tools that meet practice needs, do not overlap significantly, and deliver appropriate value. This is our story and roadmap.

We wanted to:

- Give our lawyers all of the tools they need to practice;
- Stop charging our clients for database usage (they do not like to pay for it); and
- Offer dedicated researchers for initial research to increase efficiency and improve quality.

If content can be seen as a continuum rather than a wholesale shift, we started to move along the continuum gradually, initially eliminating duplicative print and promoting and training on digital alternatives. Ultimately, we wanted to reach a point where we maintain an information ecosystem, with our users nimbly and comfortably adjusting to ongoing change and evolution into new products that deliver value in new ways.

Not about going sole provider

The world of legal information products is dominated by just a few suppliers. To appropriately evaluate and balance our resources, we knew that we needed to consider the role these major players have in our strategy. Achieving our long-term goals necessitated a strict and honest evaluation of our existing tools, especially those from our major players who reap the largest share of our budget and have the most overlapping content. In her post on *3 Geeks and a Law Blog* in 2017, Marcia Burris discussed why "Sole Provider Isn't Really a Thing".[1] Marcia suggests the view that we at White & Case share: the discussion should be around "legal research optimization" and "should include sub-points related to content (primary and secondary), efficiency of use and administration, attorney support, resource interrelatedness and content integration, cost, practice-specific needs, business needs, evolving technology, and client demands. Rather than allowing the status quo to set the tone of our discussions, let's ask what we should include as we build the law library of the future for our firms."

As we studied surveys and articles, spoke to many of our peers, and gained insights from our consultants, a number of things became evident:

- While reports ranged from 25 to 35 percent of AmLaw 200 firms currently stating they have a sole provider, firms are neutral on the selection of their supplier of choice; year-over-year growth among this group is small but persistent;

- Unsuccessful attempts to take this path appeared to be rooted primarily in moving too fast, motivated by solely cost-cutting concerns rather than a broad view to change the firm's research and information paradigms (optimizing); and
- Success rarely accompanied a "keeping up with the Joneses" mentality. While the question "What are my peers doing?" was often asked, decision-making always focused on a firm's specific needs and, fundamentally, on whether the firm still receives good value for information the major players provide relative to the cost they demand.

After considering these factors, White & Case's specific needs, and diminished value from one of our largest supplier relationships (Vendor A), we determined that the price demanded was not worth the value received. When the vendor refused to negotiate with us, we decided that to advance on the content continuum, going to a sole provider was a reasonable and compelling option to pursue as a step toward meeting our goals.

Cost as a driver

For most firms, the aggregate cost of research and information products makes the top-five list in terms of overall expense. However, given the role these tools play in producing client work, practitioners typically prefer other austerity measures, rather than drastically reducing research tools. However, early in our analysis at White & Case, we identified an unusual factor. Because clients pushed back on our recovering costs for online legal resources, lawyers deliberately sought ways to do the same research at a lower cost to the client. In other words, they avoided and used only as the last resort the content providers to whom we paid the most. To test our theory – that lawyer resource selection was based more on cost than other preferences – we instituted a six-month trial period during which our lawyers could have, in addition to the current offerings, unlimited use of one supplier (Vendor B, a competitor of our historic preferred provider) at no cost to the clients. Within days of our announcement, we witnessed a reduction of over 65 percent in Vendor A usage. Additionally, we had anticipated that lawyers would return to the paid tools for periodic access to specific resources; instead, most lawyers remained satisfied within the free environment (see Figure 1).

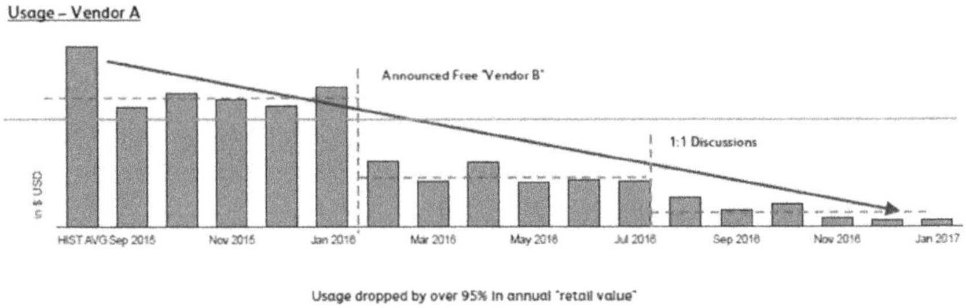

Figure 1: Effect of free service on usage of historically preferred service.

Communication is key

Consistent communication is central to managing change. Like many knowledge management (KM) change initiatives, changing research information tools is highly sensitive as it has a personal impact on most users. Kris Martin (senior director for HBR Consulting who has worked with dozens of firms on similar initiatives) consulted for us on this project, designing and helping us execute a communication plan that ensured that we communicate appropriately with the various constituencies that would be affected.

Our process began in 2015 by communicating the vision to our administrative and legal leadership team. After securing the support of leadership, we kept them in the loop by establishing a regimen for communicating key updates. As we implemented each move along the continuum, our support from leadership was reaffirmed.

Data gathering and usage analysis also played a large role in this project. Obtaining accurate user information is a critical element to understanding needs and practices and recognizing potential pitfalls. Although an initiative as far-reaching as this does require an open survey, we followed this up with direct one-on-one conversations with users. Possible solutions were refined to address both macro and individual needs.

Finally, communicating clearly with our suppliers was crucial. At no point were we unclear about our long-term strategy. We found that some (though not all) suppliers, when given information and insight into our firm's direction, adapted their content, pricing, and support to align with our long-term goals. Those are the vendors with whom we have developed strong partnerships and made longer-term commitments. When we were unable to reach that level of understanding or alignment with our suppliers, we made the difficult decision to decrease or eliminate our usage of their product over time.

Where to begin

We started with two layers of assessment. First, we conducted a survey to determine feasibility. With this light-touch approach, we incorporated financial elements such as cost and cost recovery, quantitative usage elements identifying preferences and key content sets, and qualitative inputs both from user surveys and interviews with key constituents.

These inputs allowed us to form our initial recommendations, spark dialogue with the leadership team, and obtain feedback from suppliers. Next, we did a deep dive into our actual usage to fully vet the financial impact (risk and reward), communicate with and understand specific needs from our users, and work with our consultant and suppliers to align viable solutions to our users' needs. With this layer of assessment, we finalized our recommendation and received our leadership's approval.

Successful user dialog

To get quality user input, we used HBR's methodology for customizing interviews to each user by creating change personas. For instance, users deemed to be low-risk received a simple email questionnaire as a follow-up to the survey, while higher-risk users were called directly. Personas helped to identify whether that call should come from the library, leadership, or a senior member of the user's practice. Specific details of the user's content usage helped to inform the interviewer before calling.

Indeed, leveraging a customized version of HBR's SpendConnect (a business intelligence dashboard), allowed us to quickly understand individual at a glance, anticipate areas of concern, and be prepared with tailored solutions on the call (see Figure 2). This helped make each user feel heard and able to benefit from tailored solutions.

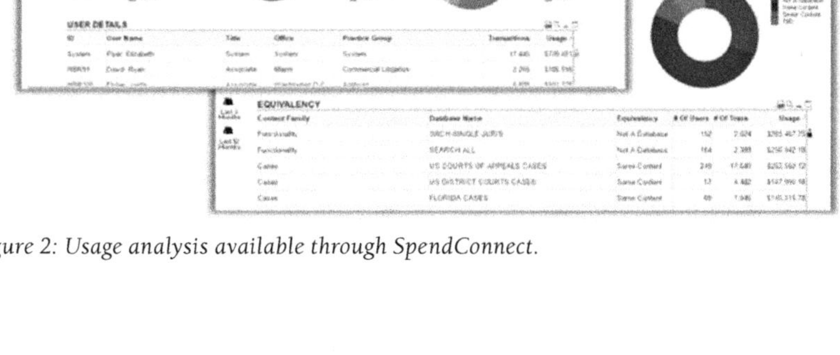

Figure 2: Usage analysis available through SpendConnect.

Our users confirmed the adage, "People don't fear change, they fear the unknown". Product familiarity was by far the greatest driver of usage. Sixty-five percent of survey respondents and over three-quarters of the people we interviewed cited familiarity as their top or only concern.

Clearly, good training is important to managing change, but equally important is allowing time for people to adopt new behaviors and ditch long-held habits.

Engaging our users in direct conversation taught us about smaller operational or technical concerns that we could address and solve, strengthening our relationships with our users. This also provided us another opportunity to communicate our mission and goals for the project.

Enhancing the toolkit

As observed above, one of our key goals was to ensure that users have the tools they need to be effective. As many of you likely have experienced, many powerful new products aimed at increasing the efficiency and effectiveness of our lawyers are on the market. Traditionally, our ability to offer these high-demand products was limited by budget. Once we released Vendor A and secured our long-term relationship with Vendor B, we could focus on enhancing our collection's value. Each law firm will find different value in the array of products out there. In our case, we added enterprise Bloomberg Law (our emerging "Vendor C"), enhancing access to practical guidance, news, analysis, data visualization tools, and market data, as well as primary and secondary law sources. We also added other innovative research and analytics tools, including CARA by CaseText, Ravel Law, and Lex Machina, all at a fraction of the cost of Vendor A, and at no cost to our clients. We knew, however, that fully leveraging these new search alternatives would require an expert team to guide and support our lawyers.

Increased user support

Our optimization project was an opportunity to not only introduce new research tools, but also to augment our research team and promote services we could not previously sustain, such as embedding researchers within practice groups. We are also using the optimization project to more actively market our library services, proactively monitor product usage, provide just-in-time training, and more fluidly navigate the wide array of product options to assure access to the best information at the lowest cost.

As Big Law increasingly finds itself competing with New Law, legal research is ripe for service transformation. The ABA survey and a study by Blue Hill Research both reveal that lawyers spend substantial time conducting legal research. While each firm draws the line between research and analysis at a different point, value comes from leveraging both efficient tools and experienced researchers.

Where do I start?

The content continuum presents a multi-year path that will differ for each firm but will represent a significant change for all. Assuring alignment with broader firm strategies, not to mention support for your overall research mission, is a critical first step. Once you have that support, define clear annual milestones with the understanding that some of these may take more than one year to accomplish. Leave time for your users to get comfortable with the alternatives.

Unless you have the rare privilege of being unconcerned with budget, as you identify new products and services that align with your mission, you will also need to make hard choices about your current collection.

Before considering eliminating one of your providers, ask yourself the following:

- Are we getting the right value?
- Is usage low, particularly among lawyers and for secondary sources?
- Can content be found elsewhere?
- Do top users and practice groups support this decision?
- Will the firm support the decision?
- Will your other supplier support the transition?
- Are external pressures, such as cost recovery or alternative fee agreements, at play?

Finally, call us or reach out to colleagues and peers who have gone down similar paths to talk about their successes or pitfalls.

Our research tools and services optimization project was the right thing for our firm, despite the challenges and effort involved. We hope analysis and discussion that we and many of our colleagues have undertaken will lead our vendors to work with us as partners, rather than insist on rigid models that are vestiges of a past that no longer supports our needs, and help us find the right solution for our firms as our needs evolve. Customers should never feel hostage to business and pricing models that are not in their and their clients' best interests, especially in times of rapid change and high pressure.

Reference

1. www.geeklawblog.com/2017/01/why-sole-provider-isnt-really-thing-and.html

Chapter 12:
Marque Lawyers – The development of law firm innovation

By Michael Bradley, managing partner at Marque Lawyers

Marque Lawyers will turn ten this year, and while we've grown and matured considerably as a business over that time, and most of us who are here now were not here at the start, our outlook has never really changed. We're having a raging debate today on what name we should give our new printer, now that its predecessor Ryan Gosling has finally died after long and faithful service. And it's the time of the week when everyone turns their mind to which song they want to nominate for the Friday playlist.

Silly, distracting wastes of time? I guess most employers would say so. But we look at the world a bit differently from most. Why is it assumed that work and play are unrelated concepts?

For us, having fun is no less serious a part of our business plan than collecting the debts (and I genuinely don't care whether or not you believe that). Quite simply, we think that those who enjoy their work, work better, and are more motivated in the long term – which is why, ten years ago, we set out to do law differently.

Marque, ten years on

Reflecting on where Marque sits in the night sky now, what I find most remarkable is how little we've changed. The firm is bigger, more materially successful, and is doing ever more interesting work for more interesting clients. We have also become increasingly sophisticated in our thinking and approach to the bigger challenges like workplace flexibility, the needs of working parents, the aspirations of Gen Y, and the perennial question of how to maintain a culture of openness and the optimistic embrace of change.

So, there is plenty happening and we haven't lost any of our enthusiasm for what's next. What I mean when I say "we haven't changed" is that we have the same values and purpose we had at the outset, and we have never felt the slightest pressure or temptation to deviate from them.

That's been revelatory. Running a business is so much more enjoyable when you know why you're doing it.

Marque's purpose, in case it needs restating, is to revolutionize the way law is practiced. Over time, we've realized that our ambitions are much greater than just finding personal happiness in the law; we aim to change the role of law and lawyers in society. We really believe we can do that. Ambitions aren't nearly so much fun if everyone else isn't telling you they're ridiculous.

The pressure of competition (or not)

Equally fascinating is the marketplace in which we've been busily going about our reinvention. I'm often asked about who we see as our competition. Has anyone been copying us? Do I think any other firm will do what we're doing? The short answer is no.

Competition is not actually something we spend any time contemplating or discussing. Not because we're so arrogant as to think that we're immune from the laws of the market; we understand the principles of marketing. It's just that law firms, like many businesses, tend to think about competitors merely as something against which to benchmark their firm – and then try to make sure they're not falling behind the trends.

That's a sure way to guarantee that you'll never innovate. The only good reason to keep an eye on your competitors is to help identify how you might differentiate your own offering. (Benchmarking, in my opinion, is a stupid pursuit.)

As to whether we're being copied or will be, our attitude is who really cares? Our most visible differentiators are the way we charge for our services and our refusal to take it all too seriously, and they're not too difficult to emulate if you want to. But the true difference cannot be replicated. We are ruthlessly authentic – honest about ourselves, sincere about everything we say, outspoken on the things we care about – and you can't copy that. You can only ever authentically be yourself. That means that Marque can't be replicated, although it doesn't mean that it can't be bettered.

So, if everyone in the legal services market isn't lying awake at night wondering how they can be more like Marque, then what is happening out there?

External forces impacting the legal market

I see three perspectives from which the state of the market can be examined: external forces; innovation in the legal market; and what the legacy firms are doing about all this. Outside of the firms, two major pressure points are gradually building. First, there is the glacial rate at which clients, particularly corporate counsel, are coming to realize just how much market power they have. The talk tends to focus on cost-cutting pressure, but that's always been a fact of corporate life and hasn't ever really impacted much on legal spend (because clients have been educated to accept that legal spend is an unknowable and unmanageable risk).

The real issue is the ability of clients to dictate to their lawyers what they will pay. I've never quite understood why this isn't more obvious to clients. It's pretty simple: with rare exceptions, the legal market is oversupplied and clients have complete mobility.

The fact is, there are plenty of good lawyers out there with the right expertise, and they're all desperate for market share. Which means that clients have enormous buying power.

As clients gain a greater appreciation of the balance of power between them and their lawyers, they will put increasing pressure on firms. At present, this tends to be focused on the meaningless quest to keep hourly rates down – meaningless because that only provides more incentives for inefficiency, over-servicing, and plain fraud. Clients do not save money by pushing rates down. (There, I said it.) The more savvy clients are taking a longer perspective on the more important questions of relationship and value. Hourly rates are a measure of cost, which ought to be irrelevant to clients. They should care less about how much it costs us to do their work, or what profit margin we get, and focus instead on the long-term value they derive for the total amount they spend. As clients place more emphasis on value, and ask ever more difficult questions about how their lawyers plan to deliver it, it will become increasingly apparent that the traditional law firm business model is ill-designed for that purpose. As it is driven solely by multiplying hours by a (made-up) figure, it focuses everyone's attention on recovering a set return for each hour. That has nothing whatever to do with the value of what each person is doing, either in the abstract or in the context of the client's needs. In the end, law firms who cling to the time costing model will be unable to effectively respond to the demands of the marketplace. They're offering the wrong service.

The second pressure point is generational. To me it's very clear that each succeeding generation is demonstrating decreasing willingness to suffer now for the promise of future gain. I readily accept that my own generation (X) largely thinks that that's just because Gen Y is "spoiled" and doesn't understand the need for hard work. I just don't agree. There's a much deeper philosophical debate to be had here. My summary of it is that the corporate paradigm which has ruled for most of the past century is now past its use-by date. The mindless pursuit of profit as an end in itself was always devoid of meaning. We all seek meaning from our lives, including from the work we do, and the younger generations are simply being noisier and more demanding about that quest. They want what they're entitled to – a sense of purpose in what they do.

Translating that to the world of law firms, consider the prospect law graduates face. A law degree has become the entry requirement into a factory job, albeit one with harbor views and gym membership. But it is a factory. Young lawyers immediately learn about the one thing which will define each day and determine their success or failure: their timesheet. Six-minute units are the measure of recognition and reward. They may get great work, impressive clients, good pay, perks, and social status. They have the prospect of promotion if they stick it out. But all of that is secondary to the absolute requirement that their timesheet is continually fed. I'm not saying that people can't derive meaning from a bargain that entails hard work, even exploitation, in return for potential future benefits. They can. Look at the acting profession. My point is that this can only really work if what is held up as of value is something that is actually of meaning to you. Nobody can derive meaning from charging hours, and yet that is how law firms measure value.

This isn't a problem with which law firms currently need to concern themselves, because there is a seemingly endless queue of hopeful new lawyers willing to accept any bargain just so they can get a start. But still, I can't see a happy long-term future for a business in which there is no alignment between the institutionalized measures of value and the human desires and needs of its workforce. (I know, salt mines can operate for many decades on exactly that basis. That's why I included the word "happy".)

Innovation in the law, or what passes for it

Turning to innovation in the legal market, legal process outsourcing (LPO) made a big splash initially. It has since been joined by technology as a serious disruptor. The role of technology is to simplify and automate legal processes and, essentially, take them out of the hands of lawyers. As artificial intelligence gains traction, it will exponentially accelerate this process.

There are many types of legal work that can be done by technology, or by LPOs or similar low-cost providers. This is the work that has always made the big law firm business model super-profitable.

The model relies on leverage – large numbers of junior lawyers and paralegals being charged by the hour at many multiples of their salaries, for what is essentially process work. The biggest earners are litigation discovery and due diligence for corporate transactions. They can be done just as effectively and many times more cheaply if outsourced. The price can also be fixed; there's no good reason for it to be charged on a time basis.

The real point here isn't so much the particular innovation being introduced, but what it is targeting. Progressively and irreversibly, all of the low-value services that law firms have traditionally leveraged for high margins are being taken away from them and captured by more efficient alternative providers. This is undermining the big firm business model.

As for the so-called "New Law" firms, good on them. Most, so far, aren't that much different from traditional firms in reality, but I think there is a positive trend towards more authentically different offerings coming to the market.

If anything has surprised me, it is the lack of willingness to do the hard work that we did, in seeking to understand the mechanisms of legal service and workplace culture, and to innovate at a fundamental level. Genuine innovation is profound; it isn't a change of logo.

Meanwhile, as Rome burns

Finally, what are the legacy firms doing? Mostly, exactly what you'd expect legacy businesses to be doing. Here's what I think we're seeing and will see more of:

- A race to the "top" – With too many big firms competing for a decreasing pool of work, they know that not all will survive. Some will respond by trying to grow to a dominant position, to ensure they are one of the survivors. Their role model for this is the victory of the Big Four accounting firms, which was achieved by constant merging and global expansion. The arrival of so many global mega firms in Australia is one indicator that numerous law firms are trying to achieve the same outcome.
- Merger mania – There's going to be a lot more of this, including some monster mergers between global behemoths.
- Poaching bonanza – The big firms have been poaching each other's big-earning partners in ever increasing numbers, and this is going to ramp up even more. The global firms have accelerated this with their deeper balance sheets, creating havoc in smaller markets like Australia.

- Fewer jobs for junior lawyers – This has been a dramatic shift in Australia; big firms have cut their graduate intake, as they narrow out their base and seek to hold on to the more profitable middle-level lawyers. It's consistent both with their push to reduce overheads and their drive towards securing more higher-level and higher-margin legal work (for which you need more senior lawyers).
- Ever more refinement of the existing business model – It ain't broke, so nobody really wants to move away from time costing. Instead, law firms are working constantly harder on squeezing every possible penny out of it.

It's a truly fascinating and exciting time to be a lawyer. Our industry is dominated by participants dedicated to refining a business model which has made them a lot of money for many years. What they're ignoring is that it became obsolete some time ago. Once you appreciate that, what looked like an overcrowded market opens up into a big field of opportunity. I'm confident that we're not the only lawyers who are seeing it. In the meantime, I have an important song choice to make.

Chapter 13:
The missing "E" in legal innovation

By John Alber, futurist at the International Legal Technology Association

Innovation talk

Cruise through the business press these days, or any number of legal industry resources, and you'll find the word "innovation" coming up often. It's become a theme of our age, and no less in law than in any other discipline.

Especially since the Great Recession, law firm clients, too, have taken up the cause of innovation – demanding that their law firms become radically more innovative in terms of pricing, unbundling, service delivery, and a host of other areas. Indeed, through organizations like the Corporate Legal Operations Consortium (CLOC) and the Association of Corporate Counsel (ACC), clients are banding together precisely to foster innovation in the firms that serve them. They're "unionizing" around these subjects, trying to accomplish by joint action what individual persuasion has failed to do over the years.

And some firms are listening. Big Law firms have recently been racing to appoint innovation partners or chief innovation officers, to field innovation committees, to feature innovation in their strategic plans, and even to create innovation-focused business units. Mid-sized and small firms, too, have heard the call and are talking up the need to innovate at partner retreats, conferences, and legal network meetings.

But is all the innovation talk inside law firms enough to initiate the wave of innovation that clients seem to want? Are we truly witnessing the advance guard of transformation in how legal services are delivered?

The simple answer is no. Firms are using the words, but even the most vocal are not taking the kinds of concrete, disciplined steps that truly innovative companies in other business sectors undertake on the way to radically innovative solutions.

The shortfall is so profound, so unlike the kind of A-student effort that lawyers typically undertake in legal spheres, that it's as though lawyers can't even spell the word innovation. They are missing the most important letter. The letter "E".

Apple innovation

To understand the point here, we'll jump industries and talk about innovation in mobile devices – an area in which, over the last decade, we've witnessed real transformation at a level that affects each of us personally. And we'll also need to transport back in time to 2006 – one year before Apple's iPhone completely altered the market for cell phones and a dozen other portable devices.

The bestselling phone in 2006 was the Motorola RAZR, a clamshell device that started out in 2004 as an expensive testament to Motorola's fashion sense. But, as Motorola dropped the price from $600 (a lot of money back then) to just a few hundred, consumers responded overwhelmingly, and Motorola found themselves with a huge success. They sold 130 million RAZRs over the life of the product. And that was a record.

How did the marketplace respond to RAZR? People marveled at its "thinness" and its "elegance". And that spawned a number of thin, elegant imitators. Here's what Avi Greengart, a prominent cellphone analyst for research firm Current Analysis said about all that:

"Fashion and thinness have become an overriding concern. Where in 2005 you might have had one or two phones that either were the RAZR or looked like it, in 2006 we now have a plethora of super-thin clamshell phones, including phones with spectacular feature sets."

Figure 1: The bestselling phone in 2006 was the Motorola RAZR...

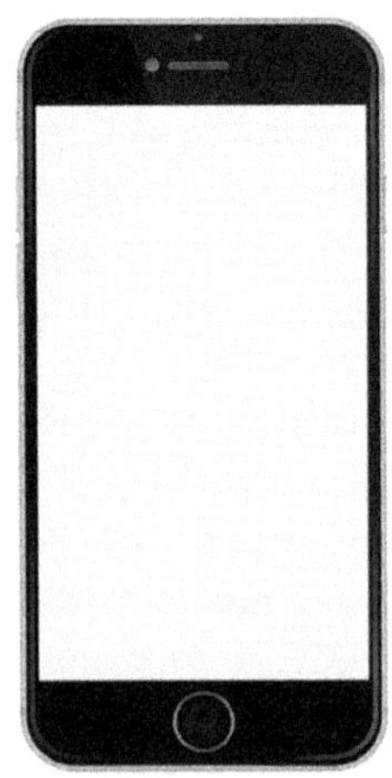

Figure 2: ...until Apple's iPhone upended the market

Among the "spectacular" features just included in the RAZR were a low-end MP3 player and a low-resolution camera. The tacked-on MP3 player was an attempt to take market share away from Apple's hugely successful iPod. Then along came Apple.

If we think about the first iPhone, we might mistake its real innovations. After all, its marvelous touch-screen interface and elegantly thin form factor did get mentioned a lot by consumers. They still do. Was Apple's success attributable simply to the fact that the iPhone out RAZRed the RAZR in terms of thinness and features?

That focus on appearance overlooks something fundamental about Apple's approach – about Apple's *process* for innovation. It was the process that shot the iPhone to the front of the market for mobile devices. Apple pursued a completely different design course from everyone else in the cellular market. In contrast with others, which often used competing design teams, Apple used the very same design team throughout its design of the Newton, the iPod, the iPhone, and succeeding mobile products. Indeed, most of the designers of the original iPhone are still on the Apple design team.

And those designers steeped themselves in Apple's and Motorola's customer base. Not only did they poll them, but they engaged them on a much deeper level, conducting focus groups, following users around as they interacted with devices, doing everything short of a Vulcan mind meld to try to put themselves not just in the shoes of their customers, but in their hearts as well. Oh, and Apple was first to implement this requirement: each member of Apple's design team had to actually use the devices they designed. They became their own user base.

Apple's design team reported directly to Steve Jobs. In many ways, he was the head of the design team. No marketing or accounting considerations stood between the team and either consumers or Apple leadership. What the design team learned about their customers' lives got reported directly up to Jobs.

Both by virtue of their long continuity with the team and their intense engagement with customers, Apple's designers came to understand those customers' needs on a deeper level than even the customers themselves did. If you had asked RAZR customers what they wanted in a next generation phone, they would have said thinner, or maybe a keyboard. Not an iPhone.

Apple's foremost lesson from its deep dive into how customers used mobile devices had nothing to do with customer-favorite feature sets or form factors. It didn't focus on thinness or fashion. Rather, it learned that the multiplication of devices, features, and functions was imposing a significant data management burden on users. Keeping track of all your music, contacts, appointments, photographs, emails, texts, messages, and other items across a range of devices was difficult for even the most savvy users. And utterly maddening for everyone else.

Thus, it wasn't Apple's elegant touch screen or polished case that caused the iPhone to surge to first among all mobile phones in just one year. It was that deep understanding of what users truly needed. Apple vaulted to the forefront in the mobile device market because, more than any other company in the market space, it was able to *empathize* with its customers and act on that understanding.

Empathy is the E in innovation. And it allowed Apple to sell as many iPhones in a quarter as Motorola sold RAZRs over the entire history of the device. By the way, it's no accident that Apple's designers are now attuned to another mobile device: the automobile. That design decision is the product of deep empathy as well.

Design thinking

The techniques that allowed Apple to conceptualize and deliver the iPhone, and that have served other product innovators so well, have been studied and written about extensively. While Apple itself has been unusually guarded about its methods, others who worked closely with Steve Jobs have distilled Apple's methods and elaborated upon them.

Those techniques, now often referred to under the mantle of "Design Thinking", have been exploding out of the design disciplines and into business, even into a small corner of the law, because they can accomplish more than is possible or likely with traditional business – or legal – methodologies.

Tim Brown, CEO of global innovation firm IDEO (with which Apple worked closely on a number of designs) and a leading proponent of Design Thinking, describes the revolution inherent in Design Thinking this way:

"Design Thinking is a human-centered approach to innovation that draws from the designer's toolkit to integrate the needs of people, the possibilities of technology and the requirements for business success."

Stanford University's Design School, which has become an open-source epicenter for Design Thinking in Silicon Valley and beyond, has distilled the elements of Design Thinking into these five tasks, as illustrated in Figure 3.

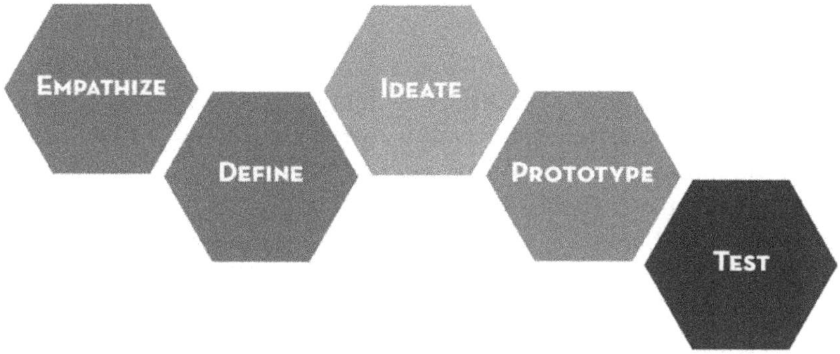

Figure 3: The Stanford d.School Design Thinking process[1]

A business using Design Thinking methods first does the sort of deep dive into customer hearts and minds that Apple did with its users. That is the Empathize phase. Then the problem is defined – as Apple did in identifying data management as a principal concern. Then ideas are spun out. But not one perfect idea at a time. Dozens of them. Even hundreds. Those are prioritized and the best of them go quickly and cheaply to some sort of prototype phase – even to paper prototypes. And those are tested with users. Then the process is repeated. Over and over and over. Iteration is essential to design. Which is to say that mistakes are also essential to design.

If we think about how most businesses, including law, design solutions to problems, we can recognize that most use far fewer than five steps in the process. Indeed, I would argue that the famously ovine legal sector uses just one: buy or try what someone else has bought or tried, and test it to see if it works. That sort of approach is certainly the genesis of many technology failures in the legal sector. They fail because they are purchasing decisions, uninformed by any of the prior design work necessary to assure that purchases are solving real and immediate problems.

It's not surprising that law firms and others short circuit process in doing service design. Empathy, the most important element of this human-centered approach to innovation, is something utterly outside the toolset given lawyers in law school. Empathy goes beyond simply trying to understand a problem. It asks you to put yourself in the shoes of the person who will use your product or service, and to try to understand that person in ways that transcend logic, that draw upon intuition and emotion as well.

Design Thinking recognizes the first-level importance of the emotional content of a successful design. When we think of traditional value propositions, we often bring to mind some notion of utility. This product or service will accomplish a certain thing. Lawyers think like that. We will provide you with advice, and it will be correct.

But the most successful designs go beyond mere utility. If you buy a Tesla, the automaker promises that you will receive the safest transportation in the world, that you will be transported in a sumptuous surround, that you will feel pampered, affluent, intelligent. In other words, the design of a Tesla is loaded with emotional content. So too with the iPhone. Its design is a response to what was often a visceral frustration with complexity. Its beautiful simplicity is directed at emotion at least as much as at aesthetics.

Clients have been telling us for years that they want more than utility in their law firms. One of the most common complaints in annual surveys about lawyers is that they take no time to understand their clients' businesses. That complaint certainly relates to the utility of advice – abstract advice is less valuable than that given in a specific business context. But the complaint also has just as much emotional content as a "you don't pay enough attention to me" statement in any other human relationship.

A new model?

What would law practice look like if it began to incorporate Design Thinking principles? What has come to be called NewLaw certainly furnishes some examples. Rocket Lawyer and Legal Zoom have recognized and responded to the deep frustration inherent in constituencies that have been priced out of traditional legal markets. Their services are easy to use, inexpensive, and for simple transactions often at least as accurate as the services provided by high street generalists. A legal consumer's reaction to the extensive document automation at the heart of those services might approximate that of the first iPhone users: "You mean I can do all this in one place? And it's easy?"

The lawyer response to such enthusiasm is often to say those tools are meant for consumer-grade legal problems. They can't possibly apply to more complex legal issues. That, unfortunately, is a typical problem-focused lawyer analysis – the kind Design Thinking circumvents. But a deeper dive into the client psyche would reveal that easier and cheaper are two of the foremost desires of clients – even sophisticated corporate clients. Lawyers are hard to reach, often unresponsive, and impose high costs on every second of interaction. Design Thinking starts with desires like that. NewLaw Design Thinking has in fact extended well beyond consumer legal transactions. For example, we tend to think of "contract automation" solutions as manifestations of AI or machine intelligence simply being redirected towards legal problems. AI may be the technology that underlies the latest contract automation products, but the fact that the problem – which has been sitting under lawyers' noses for decades – was identified at all is a clue to the existence of Design Thinking. Someone plumbed deeply the frustration and complexity inherent in managing the large numbers of contracts a global company enters into annually.

And we see, as a consequence of that inquiry, the kind of iterative design/redesign cycles in the marketplace that are the markers of real Design Thinking. As with the iPhone, when the empathy phase is done correctly, market uptake can be dramatic. And that has happened in the contract automation market.

Perhaps the most fundamental example of Design Thinking in law occurs almost completely outside the legal sector. Blockchain technology – the peer-to-peer network infrastructure that made possible cryptocurrencies like Bitcoin – was designed to support "smart contracts". These effect the tracking and transfer of digitals assets in ways that almost completely circumvent traditional legal processes. Smart contracts exist in code, not on paper, are self-enforcing without need for courts or other trusted intermediaries, and operate with orders of magnitude more efficiency, and less cost than traditional contracting processes. They are a redefinition of both money and law and an attempt at solving frustrations and inefficiencies that have long plagued traditional contracting processes. The only one who could love a traditional asset transfer – one that depended on reams of paper, inscrutable prose, antediluvian court systems, and curmudgeonly, expensive, and fussy guild workers – would be someone paid by the hour for all that trouble. No one else loves it. And blockchain is the result.

Those, such as lawyer/computer scientist Nick Szabo, who did the early work on blockchain and smart contracting, were doing a classic Design Thinking deep dive into the problems of digital commerce. What has emerged is just as iterative as the iPhone. Blockchain is certainly still in early prototype and testing stages. But billions of dollars of our clients' money is being invested to multiply the iterations until contracting is as unrecognizable to us as iPhones would have been to early 2000s cell phone users.

How many other components of our legal infrastructure are susceptible to the kind of redesign undertaken by blockchain? Certainly more than most lawyers imagine. But the threat of being designed out of existence has some firms taking a harder look at Design Thinking, and incorporating its principles into service redesign. For example, King Wood Mallesons has instituted annual 'design weeks' during which lawyers, staff, and clients take the kind of deep empathy dive contemplated by Design Thinking and try to arrive at radical new ways of delivering legal services. Other firms are beginning to send lawyers and staff off to Design Thinking "bootcamps" such as those offered by the Stanford D School.

But can firms do enough, soon enough, to participate in the revolution that seems certain to transform the law in coming decades? Here's a key differentiator between lawyer thinking and Design Thinking. Lawyers and business people want answers to questions like this. But there is no one answer to these problems. To arrive at something optimal – to an iPhone-like solution – we will have to dive deep, define goals, spin out ideas, and then prototype. And fail, then revise, then cycle through the whole process again.

Empathy, coupled with a disposition to experiment and a tolerance for failure, are the hallmarks of Design Thinking. Those are disciplines designers take for granted. But they are disciplines yet to be added to the lawyer toolkit.

It may be that enough lawyers can begin to master these disciplines, can take a real hand in the redesign of legal services that is already underway, so as to have real impact on the result. Or it may be that redesign will be left to others. In the end, we can't say what a redesigned law practice will look like. We can only say that the best answers will have been designed in all the best senses of the word. And good design is always a surprise.

Reference

1. Resources created by Hasso Plattner Institute of Design at Stanford and licensed under a Creative Commons Attribution-Non-Commercial-ShareAlike 3.0 Unported License. For more information, see: https://dschool-old.stanford.edu/groups/dresources/.

Chapter 14:
The innovation committee's brief

By Duncan Hart, barrister

To manage and grow the frequency and success of innovation-based initiatives, a structured approach is highly desirable. This enables the agenda to have continuing impact within the firm, enhance its competitive position, and produce meaningful improvements for its clients. Such an approach should involve the board creating a sub-committee (an innovation committee), tasked with the responsibility of taking such thinking firm-wide, as well as managing discreet initiatives as they arise or are deliberately explored. If the responsibility is left with the board as a whole, this is likely to impair effective and rapid response to initiatives as they arise. Boards tend to meet infrequently, have very full agendas and cumbersome bureaucratic processes; far better to have a dedicated team which has but one item on its agenda.

The committee's charter

The committee's role, authority, and reporting regime to the board should be the subject of an appropriate "charter" which defines its composition, role, responsibilities, authorities, and reporting requirements. If the firm has specific areas of strategic priority, then these should be spelled out, although they should not of course exclude other initiatives being pursued. It is often the first function of such a group to draft a charter and seek the board's approval for it. It should also provide working guidelines to indicate where the firm is seeking to innovate and indicate what broad requirements such initiatives must fulfil to attract support.

Staffing

The innovation committee is best kept to a relatively small group in relation to the size of the firm. Such appointments, while made by the board, should not be confined to board members alone; often, no more than one or two senior and influential individuals who have an interest in the area and are enthusiastic about seeing promising ideas being pursued is a wise choice. The use of external advisors, non-lawyers, and representatives from (for example) senior associate level can also be advantageous, as is the participation of clients. It is not from such appointments that the ideas must come (although this should not of course be excluded). The committee should above all be enthusiastic about the concept, have as wide an experience of commerce as possible, and be able to engender enthusiasm in others for the projects they are tasked to support. Attention to the necessity to project manage the initiatives is also a skill that should be present. Such a combination of qualities is rare; hence, the frequent need to source external members.

Creating its own initiatives and facilitating client involvement

As already mentioned, the innovation committee should be responsible for initiating innovative projects as well as supporting them when they arise. It should have the ability to initiate research into specific areas of the firm's activities, strategic priorities, and specific clients or sectors that could benefit from the creation of a specific innovation project.

It might consider, for instance, inviting clients on an ad hoc basis to address it on issues that they consider are worthy of the committee's attention, or at least indicate how they are handling similar problems in their own companies. Building relationships in this way will also ease the process of subsequently field testing innovation assumptions; clients will almost certainly be more willing to participate in such a test or pilot program. Even more importantly, they may be willing to co-partner with the firm to explore initiatives that they see may be beneficial to them. It is just this sort of approach that often leads to the creation of joint venture initiatives that seek not only to serve the specific client concerned, but are also rolled out and offered to other similar organizations.

It is in such cases that an external project manager may well be advisable to ensure appropriate expertise and rigor is brought to bear. This may be particularly useful where a specific client has agreed to become involved in a project and it is necessary to keep the project moving, coordinate resources, and ensure that processes and deadlines are met. Such a person may already be a member of the committee, but they could be sourced on a project-by-project basis.

Review and project management function

The innovation committee is tasked with making a rapid appraisal of any initiative, to offer guidance, a sponsor, and support up to a prescribed limit in the form of finance, and to provide access to resources. It must also have the capability to pull together a cross-functional ad-hoc team to assess and assist such projects at any time, particularly in its early stages.

It may either take on the role of being that project's "champion" or appoint another to the role. Once an initiative has passed a prescribed point, which may be financial or time based, and greater funding or much wider firm involvement or client involvement is desirable, then it is up to the committee to seek further resources and direction from the board. Such a committee would also have the ability, subject to its charter, to seek outside resources, involve other groups within the firm, and to conduct field testing to establish whether the idea warrants further development.

Reporting

The committee would also be primarily responsible for reporting to the board. This would involve seeking authorization and the implementation of specific initiatives across the firm's activities and, if required, incorporating the initiative into the firm's broader strategic plan, business model, and its supporting budget.

Developing an appropriate innovation mindset

The difficulty of driving innovation agendas from within organizations has become a topic of much debate. There are a number of steps that can be fostered by the committee that can assist with this.

Much of the driving force for innovation in organizations arises from those who habitually seek to collaborate to source, develop, and implement new ideas and projects. Such people are character types who are more likely to have higher degrees of empathy and what has often been described as "emotional IQ" (or EQ). In the professional services environment, this involves the need to balance the development of order (skills) and adaptability (creativity).[1] Usually, in the professional environment, the former takes precedence.

One intriguing suggestion I heard from an early-stage biotech CEO was that she biased her selection of new staff by looking for those who had been involved in starting an enterprise earlier in their careers, or at least had a family background involving small business. This would obviously exclude many lawyers who come from different backgrounds, but it does say something about the mindset that is needed in this environment.

More than traditional skills and mastering the application of those skills, it reflects the need for an understanding of the rollercoaster ride involved in new business creation, the need for risk-taking, opportunism, and networking. It is perhaps best put by Phillip Auerswald who asserts that the qualities that are most essential in today's workforce are the ability to "connect, create, contribute and collaborate".[2] The question is what steps does the innovation committee undertake to foster such qualities and enhance the creative skills demanded by their charter?

Rewards and incentives

Importantly, the committee should look very carefully at the firm's reward and promotion mechanisms that might serve to encourage this behavior. If the focus of those systems is simply to reward short-term financial results and maximize profit, the chances of meaningful engagement in innovation are lowered accordingly. Recognizing that money is a poor incentive, the firm should strive to provide meaningful ways to support and encourage innovation in its staff. Roles that recognize these skills, recognition, and continued availability for education and training in this space have an important role to play. Building one's reputation and providing meaningful work rank highly, and firms should recognize these needs at every opportunity. If the firm has in place personal and team planning and processes, then there should be clear guidelines around the role that innovation should play in developing those plans and their supporting budgets. This should be obvious at all levels within the firm from individual plans to the team's and the firm's overall strategic plan.

For decades, the key assumption that firms made concerning the behavior of employees was that if you wanted to change behaviors, the solution lay in the combined use of the carrot and stick, rewarding good behaviors and penalizing bad behaviors; the principal factor adjusted being money.

What many behavioral psychologists are now advising, however, is that while such an approach does produce results in primarily physical tasks requiring little intellectual input, it is markedly less successful where the behaviors and tasks in question fall into the more intellectual or creative areas of work.

The principal publicist of this approach is Daniel Pink[3] who has warned of the negative impact of a carrot-and-stick approach in many work environments, particularly where employees are expected to think creatively about their work and their interaction with clients. He also points out that the so-called millennials,[4] who increasingly comprise the current workforce, are looking for different work environments and rewards than previous generations.

He identifies three drivers that are far more important than either stick or carrot, particularly where millennials are concerned. He describes them as "mastery", "autonomy", and "purpose". "Mastery" is linked to the desire of an employee to become progressively better at their job, judged against that person's own standard rather than an externally set target.

"Autonomy" reflects an employee's desire to be entrusted with, and to be capable of producing, outcomes by relying on their own resources and doing it in a way and to a timetable of their own choosing. Finally, "purpose" encompasses the desire an employee has to engage though work with a range of possible "higher" aims that go beyond the success of the company or personal gain.

Such insights have major implications for those seeking to drive an innovation agenda. Encouraging and inspiring participation in "innovation project teams" presents a unique challenge for the firm's leadership team. How might such participation be encouraged, let alone rewarded?

Clearly, the autonomy of any such team can quickly be eroded by over-zealous oversight by the innovation committee or board. The availability of resources from outside the firm may, however, both satisfy the need for such a team to feel independent while providing key resources they may desperately need.

Mastery may well be satisfied by emphasizing that what is being developed through participation is a whole new set of skills that participants need to develop in order to equip themselves to face future challenges.

Many millennials have peers who themselves are increasingly attracted to start-up ventures, and therefore a firm should strive to replicate opportunities for such learning in its own environment. Not only might such experience be valued by firm members, it can also provide valuable insights to lawyers who are attempting to understand that environment and the clients of tomorrow that might emerge. Many clients in both the corporate and professional sphere are seeking to expose their employees to that experience through practical courses provided by online and consulting firms.[5]

Purpose may, however, be difficult to articulate. Where the firm focuses on providing services to socially disadvantaged or say immigrant groups, or is active in the not-for-profit sector, this may not prove such a challenge as such "higher" aims are already central to the firm's approach.

Tapping into and encouraging innovation from within established firms that are not so socially focused may therefore require the firm to realign its overall goals, or perhaps encourage innovation in particular areas of the firm's operations that can point to such a purpose. Goals espoused by the likes of Google, Facebook, and Twitter claim to provide such purpose, as evidenced by their mission statements:

- Google – To organize the world's information and make it universally accessible and useful;[6]
- Facebook – To give people the power to share and make the world more open and connected;[7] and
- Twitter – To give everyone the power to create and share ideas and information, instantly, without barriers.[8]

Attempts to espouse such objectives in the legal environment include:

- Eversheds – The global law firm that sets the standards;[9]
- Perkins Coie – Legal Counsel to Great Companies;[10]
- Cutting Edge Counsel – Legal strategies for a new economy;[11] and
- McMath Woods – To provide each of our clients with the most effective ethical representation possible, and to preserve and promote the civil justice system.[12]

Other mechanisms that permit a more or less unstructured amount of "free time" to pursue projects of their own choosing deserve consideration. Similarly, the setting up of separate entities or offsite "skunk works" to progress initiatives, as 3M do, also bears thinking about.

A longer-term answer may well arise from selective recruitment based, *inter* alia, on the applicant's background and enthusiasm for innovation. Some suggest that an applicant's background in team sports, combined with a parentage which includes self-employment, are useful markers.

Environmental scanning

In so many cases, innovations come from making unusual connections across diverse fields. Lawyers often work across very diverse industries and, if their eyes are open, they can learn much about a very wide range of commercial activities. They are often unusually well placed to connect those ideas. Innovation is often described as being the ability to combine ideas in new configurations; solutions seen in one field and then applied and/or combined with others in another.

One of the essential roles that this committee should also perform, therefore, is to constantly scan the environment for ideas, technologies, and innovations that are being developed outside of the firm. Lawyers, particularly those on secondment to clients, should also be requested to contribute their observations and be briefed accordingly before commencing their secondments. Their purview should not be restricted to looking only at law firms, but across the whole range of industry, both in their own country and outside it.

Many ideas developed for quite disparate applications can have a useful role to play, if properly adapted, within law firms and in their relationships with their clients. This includes not only the building of technology-focused solutions, but also differing business models or systems that might have an application. One firm I worked with had adapted the "loyalty" points process to encourage repeat business; another utilized a franchise model to extend a very specific offering through a network of other law firms.

Educational and promotional activities

The committee should also take on the responsibility for ensuring that its role as well as its activities and appropriate training and resources are disseminated throughout the firm and incorporated into its wider processes – e.g. recognition and reward mechanisms, recruitment induction and wider training programs, participation in firm seminars, client surveys etc. For this reason, its wider role will require the active involvement of the firm's marketing, financial, and HR resources who should be involved in the committee's deliberations if not formally members of that committee.

Summary of support functions

In Table 1, I have summarized the nature of support mechanisms that can be introduced by the innovation committee, related in part to the nature of the innovation. Firms should not shy away from engaging as widely as possible across a spectrum of external advice and guidance in order to build its own agenda. Professional service firms have much to learn from other industries and their own journeys in this space and they should not hesitate to search it out and borrow extensively.

Internal team management and client liaison – The politics

Finally, almost every innovation will or should involve a high level of both internal firm liaison and client or potential client interaction. This will inevitably require close coordination with the partner responsible for such client(s) and, given the protective nature of some partners to "their" clients, this will require careful management by the sub-committee, as well as support from the ownership structure of the firm.

Negativity or obstruction from partners who may not share enthusiasm for the committee's aims is a very probable roadblock in many firms and can quickly dissuade otherwise enthusiasts for the project

	All innovation	'Legal' innovations	Incremental	Transformative/ disruptive
Support				
Recruitment and training				
Selective recruitment	✔	✔	✔	✔
Training & secondment	✔	✔	✔	✔
Mentoring (Internal)	✔	✔	✔	✔
Mentoring (External)	✔	✔	✔	✔
Leadership and structure				
Innovation agenda	✔	✔	✔	✔
Board innovation sub-committee	✔	✔	✔	✔
Innovation champion/leader	✔	✔	✔	✔
Peer review process		✔		✔
External consultants				✔
Incubator group				✔

Table 1: Supporting an innovation agenda

to lose commitment. The committee must take every opportunity to provide the necessary backing and authority to remove such roadblocks and not leave it up to the individual project teams to negotiate what they might see as career-threatening obstacles raised by such partners. In short, they must run "interference" for their project teams when occasion demands it!

Creation of "off campus" options

Many have speculated that the ability of firms to successfully innovate is fraught with difficulties as new initiatives fight to prove themselves and, to many within the firm, appear to claim an "unfair" share of resources.

Even worse, any substantial innovation of the transformational or disruptive kind can be very threatening to those who are well looked after within the current model. In short, they do not enjoy being seen as "yesterday's heroes", particularly when it is that current model that is still bringing home the bacon and subsidizing the more speculative innovation agenda.

Thus, established firms often consider the merits of developing and housing more transformational initiatives off campus and establish entirely new administrative and organizational entities to take the project forward. This was IBM's solution when it sought to enter the PC market and cannibalize its main frame business, then the dominant money maker of the business. Similarly, the creation of Riverview Law by DLA Piper in the UK was a deliberate decision, which also enabled the creation of an entirely separate brand with different pricing, market etc. Such an approach has also been seen in GMH's development of its Saturn brand and Toyota with Lexus.

Buying innovation – Was it the product or the people?

Few firms can expect their innovation agenda to be driven exclusively from within. It is very common practice now to find that most companies will set aside funding and resource to acquire promising innovations well before they have been proven in the market. This requires close attention to such sources of insight as the investment community, incubators, venture capital firms, and angel groups. This not only provides the opportunity to "get in on the ground floor", but is also a rich source of ideas and techniques to assist the committee in managing its own program, sourcing external expertise etc. Firms such as Allens Linklaters, PwC, and Deloitte – and no doubt many others – are either active organizers, participants, or are formally associated with "incubators or accelerators" for this reason.

Integrating or exploiting such early stage initiatives from outside the firm is thus a key capability that the committee must also develop, and it should be a regular feature of their report to the leadership team. Companies such as Google, Apple, and Yahoo regularly pay very high prices for promising start-ups, recognizing that even at the price they pay, these products would cost much more if developed internally, assuming of course that had been likely in the first place. In some cases, the innovations concerned are not as important as the recruitment of the personnel associated with the development of that particular product or service. What is sought is to acquire people and their demonstrated ability to create and bring an innovation to market. Again, careful questions need to be asked about the ability to integrate such initiatives, let alone personnel, into your existing firm, and whether or not the group concerned is better retaining its separate identity under the umbrella of the firm but subject to its own rules.

A good example of this approach has been the development and deployment by some of the major firms of separate corporate identities which are tasked with creating a pool of skilled lawyers. These lawyers are to be available for relatively short-term assignments, can be added to the firm's workforce in the event of sudden demand for additional personnel, and can be seconded to the firm's existing clients. Examples include the creation of Orbit by the Australian firm Corrs, and Peerpoint by Allen & Overy. Such entities benefit from the backing of well-known and established firms. They are designed to compete with standalone entities, such as AdventLaw, who have entered the market in recent years to fill the demand, mainly driven by in-house corporate counsel, for additional resources at cheaper rates than can be provided by their usual legal providers.

In such cases, the need to employ fresh resources, and for the new entity to develop its own culture, is strongly suggested given the speed and flexibility that the new service might require. It may also be essential to recruit for different skills and attitudes as the new venture grows. It is unlikely that from the existing ranks of the old firm there will be sufficient qualified candidates to staff the needs of the new organization. This, in fact, may prove to be a fundamental problem in getting an innovation strategy off the ground initially and may cause the committee to adopt a more externally resourced strategy to not only drive your innovation efforts, but to "house" them if the initiative shows sufficient promise.

It may also occur that an individual or a group who are proponents of an innovation feel sufficiently strongly about it to want to leave the firm and pursue it separately, the firm having perhaps decided it was not for them at the time. Again, this must be expected and, in such a situation, the firm could adopt what I am told is CISCO's approach. CISCO apparently offer seed funds to such a departing person to develop the initiative, provided that at CISCO's option those funds can be converted into equity, should CISCO so choose within say a five-year period. This could be combined with possible options to purchase additional equity.

Sourcing external funding – Private equity, joint ventures, and the stock market

One of the major impediments to innovation is the lack of funds with which to fuel and launch the initiatives it might come up with. This is aggravated by the traditional partnership model where retained profits are treated as taxable income in the hands of partners, and thus retention is a very unpopular option by which to fund innovation. While this is often heard more as an excuse for lack of activity in this area, there is no doubt that funds available from external sources often provide the incentive for action and are accompanied by demands that those funds be applied in more innovative and profitable projects.

This had often resulted in the more predictable path of funding acquisitions (e.g. the 2007 ASX float of Slater & Gordon[13]), but increasingly such funds are being made available through private equity (Legal Zoom), or by listed companies taking an ownership stake in law firms as is permitted in Australia and the UK. The size of the legal industry, its profits, and the loosening of regulatory restrictions almost guarantees this will be the case. IT-delivered solutions, such as Legal Zoom and numerous imitators as well as more flexible "virtual" firms, will also drive this process and attract capital. In the area of IP, for instance, companies such as Inovia and CPA Global will also act as drivers of innovation funded by capital seeking to maximize its return in what is seen as a sector ripe for disruptive change and offering high profitability. The float of Sprusons/IPH in Australia in late 2014 is further recent evidence.

In the Sprusons case, a firm with a turnover of approximately A$80 million sold half the equity of the firm for A$160 million to fund its expansion both within Australia, but more particularly in Asia. Developing significant IT systems, expansion into China, and potential acquisitions were a central part of its pitch to the market and were driving the need for additional access to funds. Significantly, they also highlighted the ability to attract and retain staff through what amounted to deferred option rewards as a significant reason for becoming a listed entity.

One can expect, therefore, that if change is not driven from within a firm's own innovation agenda, then better funded and externally driven competition will likely force the need for change up any firm's agenda in any event. The lessons from Silicon Valley are clear. Professional service firms have a limited window in which to explore and develop their skills and to build their capability to develop and manage their "innovation agendas". The availability of outside funding, the pressure to differentiate, and client demands will require every firm to address this key issue. Innovation, as we have seen, encompasses a wide range of activities and no aspect of any firm's operations should be seen as immune from its particular demands.

Purely "legal" innovation must also be supported

Much recognition is often given to what I have described as "legal innovations". Such recognition arises most commonly because the firm concerned has overcome what appeared to be insuperable obstacles to a particularly complex deal being done. Alternatively, it may represent a new solution to resolving a long-standing problem, or running a contentious case to establish "new law", often to the benefit of its wider client base. The possibilities are clearly endless, but the rewards are exceedingly high in kudos to the firm, attraction or retention of clients, and often by way of contingency or "uplift" fees being paid.

Again, the emphasis should be upon raising a number of such potential issues to solve and then testing their relative importance with clients in order to assess those most likely to result in favorable client response.

Defining and pursuing a class action, defending an industry sector from new government regulation, and protection of assets from compulsory acquisition are all potential areas where an innovative approach might be warmly applauded by clients.

The committee should therefore be alert to, and regularly consider encouraging, such initiatives. The wider the potential benefits, particularly where large industry sectors are involved, the better. In such cases, it may well be that an appropriately engaging social issue is at stake which will energize some members of the firm to more active engagement and satisfy the need for there to be a higher "purpose" than merely profit in evidence.

References

1. Auerswald, P. E., *The Coming Prosperity: How Entrepreneurs are Transforming the Global Economy*, Oxford University Press, 2012.
2. Ibid.
3. www.danpink.com
4. Approximately, those born between 1980 and 2000 and now firmly established in the global workforce.
5. See the author's participation in such a course, 'Lean Innovation for Lawyers', at www.leaninnovation.com
6. www.google.com/about/company
7. newsroom.fb.com/company-info
8. about.twitter.com/company
9. www.eversheds.com/global/en/who/about-us/our-approach.page
10. www.perkinscoie.com/en/index.html
11. cuttingedgecounsel.com
12. www.mcmathlaw.com
13. S&G have made over 50 acquisitions

www.ingramcontent.com/pod-product-compliance
Ingram Content Group UK Ltd.
Pitfield, Milton Keynes, MK11 3LW, UK
UKHW022012141025
3285IPUK00007B/98